How To Make
A Meatball

Recipes For Living My Mother Taught Me

MA

ISBN: 0996457402
ISBN 13: 9780996457408

This book is dedicated to my parents,

Joseph and Molly Bruno

I lived a life of joy and security and love and Jesus because of the way you both lived your lives.
I love you.
I always will.

A SPECIAL LOVE FILLED THANK YOU TO

My husband, Phil Armenia for sharing this life with me for forty-six years. Your care for my parents in their final years has been something beyond love. It has been like Jesus Himself loving them and having compassion that comes from heaven itself. Thank you. And thank you for always and utterly encouraging me to be the woman God created me to be.

My son, Philip and my daughter-in-law Renee for loving me unconditionally. I am so proud of who you are. I love you.

My grandchildren, Allie, Michael and Rachel for the joy that comes from being "Mema." That you are the three most perfect human beings alive on earth today is utter and unchangeable truth.

Ivey Harrington Beckman for giving a wife and mother who wanted to be a writer the chance to be one for the last twenty-two years. Thanks also for the editing of "Meatball" and for loving my mom and for loving me. I love you.

Brenda Harris for loving Molly Bruno and for loving me. Thanks for the constant encouragement to write and keep writing, and for the gentle way you edit my words in this book. I love you.

Wanda Geddie Brickner who, while a magazine was doing a cover story about her, suggested to Ivey Harrington Beckman, the editor, that she might want to consider her friend, Marie, as a writer for the magazine. Ivey said, "Sure" and kept using my writing for over two decades. Thank you, Wanda for giving me the open door to walk through. I love you.

Rev. Michael and Maria Durso for all these decades of your steady support –through good times and not-so-good times. The powerful presence of the Holy Spirit in your lives, in your words and in your actions has been a constant reminder that Jesus is alive and He loves His children. His love in you has been poured on us. I love you.

Rev. Daniel and Vangie Mercaldo for loving us, guiding us, caring about us and being our pastor no matter where we live. We love you.

Finally, and most importantly I want to thank my heavenly Father for being so kind and merciful to me. I pray that as this book lifts up Jesus, the power of The Holy Spirit will make Him real and alive to the reader, because He is real and alive.

July 14, 2015

INTRODUCTION

THE WORK OF MEATBALLS

"So, you're saying I should change the title of my book?" I asked my husband.

"Well, I don't know about that," Phil replied, "but if you write a book about the lessons your mother taught you, and title it *How to Make a Meatball*, then you are, in essence, referring to yourself as the meatball your mother made."

"Phil, *How to Make a Meatball* is a metaphor for how my Italian-American mother taught me to overcome, thrive, and live joyfully on this planet."

"You're missing my point, Marie," Phil said. "Describing someone as a *meatball* can mean that individual is unintelligent, dull, or fat. It's never a compliment."

"I'm not missing your point, Phil, you're missing the analogy. Making a meatball is analogous to my mother's philosophy and faith about living a victorious, joyful, and fulfilling life."

Phil tried another approach.

"Urban Dictionary says that when you call someone a *meatball* you're calling that person unintelligent, dull, or fat."

"Well, Phil, am I unintelligent, dull, or fat?" (After 45 years of marriage, I know the right questions.)

"Anything but, Marie!" (After 45 years of marriage, my husband knows the right answers.)

"You've eaten many of my mother's meatballs, correct?"

"Yes, they're the best."

"And you've eaten my meatballs, the ones my mother taught me how to make, correct?

"Yes, they're great."

"I rest my case."

And thus ended the discussion about the title of this book and whether or not I'm calling myself a meatball.

I'm not.

Or am I?

The Work of Meatballs

My family tree is deeply rooted in Italy, but I didn't grow up in Naples crushing grapes with my feet. I'm a third-generation American who grew up walking the concrete of New York City, surrounded by the love of a robust Italian-American family — and lots and lots of food, including homemade meatballs.

When I was a child, moms did most of the cooking. This could be why so many mothering metaphors relate to food items. Think about two of the most spoken: "as homemade as apple pie" and "that's chicken soup for the soul." Apple pie is basic and sweet. Chicken soup is warm and comforting. Mom stuff.

However, when I think of my mother, I envision hot, juicy meatballs bubbling around in a huge pot filled with tomato sauce and Italian sausage. My mother, Molly Bruno, is the Michelangelo of meatball making. Just thinking of the aroma that wafts from her meatballs makes my mouth water. As an Italian-American, I believe that the meatball is a radically underappreciated food. Why? Meatballs take a lot of work and time.

A great meatball is created from a bunch of ingredients — and so is a person, which is why my metaphor holds together. It's like a potter putting the clay on a wheel to form it into something better than just a lump of clay. God transforms us from what we were and makes us into something better and far more desirable to those around us.

So, how do you make a meatball, metaphorically speaking? It's not rocket science, but it does take some know-how.

Step One

You must soften the meat. This may seem like a brutal process to an inexperienced observer — to crush and grind the meat — but it's the only way to make it pliable enough to form a meatball. Softening it so that it can be made into something new is the whole point.

God does the same thing with our hearts. We know we feel dead inside. Our hearts are like stone. He gives us new hearts. He softens them, and the process, though crushing at times, transforms us into new creatures.

"I will give you a new heart and put a new spirit in you; I will remove from you your heart of stone and give you a heart of flesh."

— EZEKIEL 36:26

Step Two

A meatball must be seasoned, and salt is the primary seasoning. I don't know why salt gets first place, but it does. A meatball without salt is a meatball without flavor. And if a meatball has no flavor, what good is it?

Salt gets little respect in the seasoning world. In recent decades, we've discovered how to mine salt inexpensively, which is why you never see a salt charge on a restaurant menu.

But salt wasn't always so easy to get. Throughout history, it was so expensive to mine that people referred to it as "White Gold."[1] Some historians tell us that Roman soldiers were paid in salt. The word *salary* is actually derived from the Latin word *salarium,* which means payment in salt. [2].

In the Old Testament, salt was used to seal covenants. God gave the *"kingship of Israel to David and his descendants forever by a covenant of salt"* (2 Chron.13:5). God also required salt in some offerings: *"Every offering must be seasoned with salt, because the salt is a reminder of God's covenant"* (Lev. 2:13, TLB).

Salt is a reminder of God's covenant? That's what Scripture says. And Christians are now the "salt of the earth"? That's what Jesus said. Our lives are the salt reminding the world around us that Jesus offered Himself as our offering to God. Christians who have been given and have received new hearts, represent a new covenant that began with the ultimate sacrifice of Jesus on the cross. We are the salt that reminds the world that God is willing to forgive, forget, and welcome them into His forever family. And to resurrect us when we die.

A meatball without salt is tasteless, and so is the world without The Body of Christ. Jesus was saying something amazing, priceless, and beyond human comprehension when He told His followers:

"You are the salt of the earth."

— MATTHEW 5:13

Step Three

But meat and salt do not a meatball make. The meatball maker must add extra ingredients (milk, bread, eggs) to keep a meatball pliable — and to keep it from falling apart when it hits the hot oil.

God gives us new hearts with new life, and then His plan is to make us look like His Beloved Son, Jesus. When God works to form us into the image of His Son, Jesus, He adds the ingredients we need to keep us soft-hearted, and He adds ingredients that will keep us from falling apart when life gets, well, hot. We cannot make it through the troubles of life on mental discipline alone. We need something formed within us, something that becomes part of who we are in our inner being. We need something new, miraculous, and holy. We need something that will help others see Jesus walking with us and working in us so that we begin to resemble who He is. We need The Holy Spirit. We need what He cultivates in us.

"The fruit of the Spirit is love, joy, peace, forbearance, kindness, goodness, faithfulness, gentleness and self-control."

— GALATIAN 5:22-23

Step Four

Next, the meatball maker works all the ingredients together until the mixture is ready to be formed into a meatball. A genuine meatball maker knows mixing the meatball is a hands-on process. Our heavenly Father is a hands-on loving Father with every one of His children.

Since each of us is an original creation of God, He's hands-on from the moment He gives us life in the womb. King David acknowledged this, saying, *"For you created my inmost being; you knit me together in my mother's womb...My frame was not hidden from you when I was made in the secret place, when I was woven together in the depths of the earth. Your eyes saw my unformed body..."* (Ps.139:13,15-16).

But we also learn from David that God is with us for more than just the moments of our creation. In the same Psalm, David described God's hands-on involvement in his daily life when he said to God, *"You have searched me, LORD, and you know me. You know when I sit and when I rise; you perceive my thoughts from afar. You discern my going out and my lying down; you are familiar with all my ways. Before a word is on my tongue you, LORD, know it completely"* (Ps. 139:1-4).

Our Creator knows us better than we know ourselves. David explained this in Psalm 139:7. *"Where can I go from your Spirit? Where can I flee from your presence?"*

When God created me, He saw me writing this book. When He created you, He saw you reading it today. In Psalm 139:16, David reminded us of God's hands-on involvement in every aspect of every person's life. *"Your eyes saw my unformed body; all the days ordained for me were written in your book before one of them came to be."* God is the original hands-on Creator. His hands never leave us.

"Your right hand will hold me fast."

— Psalm 139:10

Step Five

At this stage of the meatball-making process, it's time to apply the heat and the oil. A great meatball is soft inside and firm on the outside. The exterior crust is necessary or the meatball will simply disappear into the sauce.

One of my favorite Bible stories is that of Shadrach, Meshach, and Abednego. These three men faced a literal fire because they would not bow down and worship the golden image King Nebuchadnezzar had made.

I love the all-or-nothing attitude of these men when they said, *"If we are thrown into the blazing furnace, the God we serve is able to deliver us from it... and... even if he does not, we want you to know, Your Majesty, that we will not serve your gods or worship the image of gold you have set up"* (Dan. 3:17-18).

Shadrach, Meshach, and Abednego were my childhood superheroes. Stop and think about all the people who *did* bow down to the golden image even though they knew they were compromising God's Law. Almost everyone compromised their commitment to God. These cowering people saw God greatly honor and deliver the three men who stood their ground.

But by no means did Shadrach, Meshach, and Abednego walk through the hot fire alone. Jesus was there walking in the fire with them. King Nebuchadnezzar saw Him with his own eyes. And when Shadrach, Meshach, and Abednego exited the fire at the King's command, *"Their hair wasn't singed, their robes were not scorched and there was no smell of fire on them"* (Dan. 3:27).

People who can take the heat are people who are not afraid of the future because they know that God already has a plan in place for every day of their lives. Jesus told us that the world would hate us because He has chosen us, and because we love him (John 15:18-19). He wants us to persevere and stand our ground — even when life gets hot — and He is with us every step of the way.

"I have told you these things, so that in me you may have peace. In this world you will have trouble. But take heart! I have overcome the world."

— JOHN 16:33

"...When you walk through the fire, you will not be burned; the flames will not set you ablaze."

— ISAIAH 43:2

Step Six

Finally, although a meatball is *in* the sauce, it is not *of* the sauce. It never loses its separate identity. It never becomes the sauce, no matter how much the sauce surrounds it. The meatball maker never intends for the meatball to give up its new and unique identity and be lost in the sauce.

When God creates a new heart in us, we take on a new and eternal identity, even while we continue to live in the same place we've always lived. We are *in* the world but we are not *of* the world. The apostle Paul explains it this way: *"...anyone who belongs to Christ has become a new person. The old life is gone; a new life has begun!"* (2 Cor. 5:17, NLT). *"Do not conform to the pattern of this world, but be transformed by the renewing of your mind. Then you will be able to test and approve what God's will is – his good, pleasing and perfect will"* (Rom. 12:2).

Something About Molly

All this talk of meatball-making brings me back to my mother. For most of my adult life, people have been encouraging me to write a book about Mom. She's hilarious, filled with God's power and love. She prays for people and gets answers to her prayers. She's a nuclear-powered witnessing machine.

Everyone (and I mean *everyone*) who meets my mother falls in love with her. I'm repeatedly told how blessed I am to have her.

But lots of people have mothers their friends adore. They don't necessarily write books about them. So why am I writing one? What changed? Well, the world did. These days, more women, for a variety of reasons, are focusing less on careers and more on the basics of being someone's mother.[3] And many of them have no personal example to follow. Their moms were career-minded mothers who believed prioritizing the roles of a wife and mother was not necessary. So, they didn't. And now, the daughters of those mothers have become wives and mothers. And they're desperately trying to figure out how to do it right. How do I know this? The Internet.

A quick review of the top ten blogs[4] written by and for women reveals that the focus is on traditional subject matter: marriage, childbirth, parenting, cooking, fashion, and crafts. Conduct an Internet search for the word *mentor* and you'll discover that the business world is adopting the process

God created for women all along: find someone who has been there and done that, listen to their advice, and follow that person's example (Titus 2:4).

God created the mentoring system and has kept it in place for thousands of years Jesus said that His life on earth was an example for us to follow (John 13:15). The apostle Paul took it a step further when he wrote, *"Follow my example, as I follow the example of Christ"* (1 Cor. 11:1).

In that spirit, I offer my mother's life as an example for younger women to follow. She is, as I write this, 92 years old, so almost anyone who picks up this book is a younger person.

Why the Church is on the Outs

Traditionally, the church is the place where women have been more likely to find older, godly mentors who will obey God's call to be an example to others. However, our daughters and granddaughters (and their husbands and children) are leaving the organized church in droves. Barna Research confirms "nearly six in ten (59 percent) of young people who grow up in Christian churches end up walking away from either their faith or from the institutional church at some point in their first decade of adult life."[5]

Why the mass exodus? The answer may surprise you. The Barna report states, "When comparing twenty-somethings who remained active in their faith beyond high school and twenty-somethings who dropped out of church, the study uncovered a significant difference between the two: those who stay were twice as likely to have a close personal friendship with an adult inside the church. Seven out of ten Millennials who dropped out of church did *not* have a close friendship with an adult and nearly nine out of ten never had a mentor at the church."[6] The Barna study proves that older people mentoring younger generations is a simple system created by a God who knows what works with people and why.

The more the world seems out of control, the more people are desperate to connect with someone who has lived life with a strong and steady faith. My mother is such a person. Her anecdotes about answers to prayer and her unmitigated witnessing wherever she goes so charmed a friend of mine that she told her employers, who are movie producers, about Mom. They were interested in speaking to Mom because they were creating a character in their next movie — an older, praying woman who mentors a younger woman. We set up a Skype session with Mom and the movie producers. They used her life as a character study for their movie character.

Mom loves talking to people who want to talk to her about Jesus. Anything about her life that may cause another person to love God more is her primary goal before she sees Jesus. And seeing Jesus is Molly Bruno's ultimate goal. And that is another reason I chose to write this book at this moment in time. I want Mom to read it before she sees Jesus.

And I want you to read it before you see Him too.

1

THE MEATBALL DOESN'T FALL FAR FROM THE POT

The Recipe For Being Real

"Her children arise and call her blessed."

— Proverbs 31:28

Four minutes before the sniper started shooting at my mother from the roof of the house next door, she was sitting at the kitchen table in our New York City home, reading the newspaper. I was 15 years old and had just gotten home from a youth group meeting at church. I kissed Mom "hello" and went to my room to change my clothes.

We both knew the ritual that would follow: I'd find my way back to Mom, where I would talk non-stop about every detail of my evening. Long before she was finished listening, I would be finished talking. My Mom's patience says a great deal about her motherly love and listening skills because, trust me, I can talk!

When I was finished telling her every single detail of my night, Mom would hug me, pray for me, kiss me on my face a few times, and then we would both go to bed. On the night in question, my father, always an early riser, was already asleep. Mom and I had no way of knowing how different that night would be.

When I opened my bedroom door four minutes later, the house was completely dark. Through the utter darkness, I heard Mom whisper loudly, "Marie, don't turn on the light! Get down on the floor. Someone is shooting at me from the roof of the house next door!"

"Whaaaaaaaat?"

"Get down! Get down! There's a sniper shooting at me!"

I hit the floor. A sniper? Shooting at my mother? It was the late 1960s. Our country was being shocked every day with more and more violence, assassinations, street protests, and every kind of disorder. And, obviously, on that night, it had reached our home on Wadsworth Avenue.

Mom was hunched on the floor underneath the kitchen window. I crawled over to where she was kneeling. She carefully pulled back a tiny corner of the crisp, freshly starched curtain and pointed to a spot on our neighbor's roof.

"See the rifle?" she whispered.

I definitely saw the rifle.

I assumed that behind the rifle, hiding in the shingled darkness of our neighbor's roof, lurked an unseen psychopathic killer targeting my meatball-making mother. But why, why, why?

"Let's go get Daddy!" I suggested.

My father, a pastor at the time, is a dignified, elegant, intelligent, and highly respected man who would certainly know what to do about a sniper shooting at his wife and daughter. My mother disagreed.

"No!" Mom protested, "Let's call the police! He's also shooting at the cars on the highway at the end of our backyard!"

Mom crawled on her hands and knees to the kitchen wall phone to put in a call to NYPD (New York Police Department).

I sat frozen with fear and listened as Mom said, "Officer, this is Molly Bruno. There's a sniper on the roof of the house next door (long pause). Yes, a sniper. He's shooting at me and at the cars on the highway behind our house. Thankfully, the Lord protected me."

Even under duress, Mom never missed a chance to give glory to God for His faithfulness. She gave the police officer necessary details: our address, phone number, and the address of the house next door. When she finished her emergency call, we both crawled to the bedroom to wake my father.

She woke him with nightmarish sentences.

"Honey! Wake up! A sniper almost killed your wife tonight! He's shooting at me and the cars on the highway from the roof of the house next door!"

Dad sat straight up in bed — poor man — and said, "Whaaaaaaaat?"

He then jumped out of bed and crawled on his hands and knees into the kitchen, as my mom suggested for his safety.

Watching my distinguished father crawl through the house on all fours heightened my sense of being in a terrifying crisis.

Once again, mom pulled back the same tiny, crisply starched corner of the kitchen curtain. She pointed to the sniper, saying, "See? There he is. There's his rifle!"

My father replied, "Where? I don't see a rifle."

"Right there," she pointed, "right there at the corner of the roof."

"You mean that thing moving back and forth?"

"Yes."

"That's not a rifle, Hon. It's the branch of a tree."

"It is?"

Mom and I took another look at the "sniper" on the roof. Either the sniper had some kind of secret power that allowed him to instantly transform himself from a Molly-targeting psychopathic sniper into an innocent tree branch — or we saw an innocent tree branch and assumed it was a Molly-targeting psychopathic sniper. We went with the innocent branch theory.

"Ohhhh," Mom and I said in unison, our mouths open wide with disbelief at our hilarious blunder.

My dad was smiling when he said, "Never a dull moment around this house." He then went back to bed.

Mom and I hugged each other while uttering peals of breath-robbing laughter.

"How funny!" we said to each other, "It must have been a car backfiring on the highway."

It was all fun and laughter for a minute or two, until reality banged on the front door of our brains and reminded us that the NYPD was on its way to storm our neighbor's house. I wondered: *Are they going to bring a S.W.A.T. team?*

Mom ran back to the wall phone, redialed the NYPD, and confessed her visual blunder.

"Officer, this is Molly Bruno calling back. I just called about the sniper on the roof. You know what? It was a tree branch, not a sniper (long pause). No, you are correct. I should have checked before calling. Please forgive me for bothering you. The Lord bless you."

If you know anything about the NYPD, they will give their lives to protect their citizens — but not necessarily from tree branches. The officer wasn't happy with my mom.

Three minutes later, Mom peeled back the same corner of the kitchen curtain, and we watched a police cruiser stop in front of our neighbor's house. Mom and I held our breath as the police officers remained inside the car. After a few minutes, the cruiser drove away, and our neighbors were none the wiser about what almost happened.

And that night we added "The Sniper Story" to a long list of stories in which my mother is the holy and hilarious central character.

Because "The Sniper Story" Is Hilarious, That's Why

Some people might not start a book about lessons they learned from their mother with a whacky story about how she called NYPD to report a tree limb shooting at her. Other people in other families might keep that story a secret filed under "embarrassing life bloopers." I suspect, however, that those people don't know the freedom of having a mother who taught them that the biggest mistake a person can make in life is believing they will never make a mistake.

But in my family, it makes perfect sense that if you have a zany story about calling NYPD to report a tree branch shooting at you, you most definitely should tell it again and again, laughing while you do.

A few years after the sniper incident, I married my high school sweetheart, who became a pastor. During that season of my life, I saw firsthand the incredible gift my mother gave me when she taught me to accept that I would make mistakes now and then. I observed in others that the unreasonable pressure to live a mistake-free life has the ability to destroy a human heart as completely as any sin, addiction, or weakness. A terrified child lives inside many troubled adults who somehow got the message that mistakes are final. I met many fearful Christians who were convinced that from the moment they gave their lives to Jesus, God expected them to be perfect in every way. They didn't seem to be able to grasp that God had hidden them and their imperfection in the perfection of Jesus Christ.

When I told Mom I was writing this book about the lessons she taught me, she had three stipulations: "Make sure the glory goes to God and not to me; don't make it look like I'm perfect; and don't be fake about anything you write."

I will do my best, Mom.

Don't Argue With God

> "What sorrow awaits those who argue with their Creator. Does a clay pot argue with its maker? Does the clay dispute with the one who shapes it, saying, 'Stop, you're doing it wrong!' Does the pot exclaim, 'How clumsy can you be?' How terrible it would be if a newborn baby said to its father, 'Why was I born?' or if it said to its mother, 'Why did you make me this way?'"
>
> — ISAIAH 45:9-10

Before my mother taught me one thing about *what to do* in life she taught me *who to be*: myself. Just be myself.

Being fake is almost the unpardonable sin in my mother's world. She believes doing that is giving God the unspoken message that you don't like His work. Who has the nerve to tell God He did a bad job at anything? Mom's advice? It's better to have one friend who loves the real me than a thousand friends who prefer a fake version. This relieves a great deal of pressure (peer pressure and otherwise) when you're looking for that one friend who "gets" you.

Molly Bruno isn't a fake cheerleader of a mom who is convincing her daughter to love herself. It's a spiritual issue for her. Her deep conviction about this stems at the most basic level from her reverence and submission to God and His sovereignty. According to Mom, the way God created each one of us is His business, not ours. If a woman goes through life arguing with God about something as basic as the way He created her, she'll never learn to trust Him and His ways. And if a woman doesn't learn to trust God and His ways, nothing else she accomplishes in life really matters.

Science can explain to us the process of creating a human being, but Scripture tells us that is it God who knits each of us together in our mother's womb (Ps. 139:13). Who is the One who controls that DNA? Who made the split second decisions when your DNA chain was being created? The Bible says it was God; therefore, so does my mother.

I Love You Just The Way You Are

Not only did Mom teach me to accept myself the way God made me, but **she** accepted me the way God made me. I cannot recall throughout all my many decades of life ever hearing Mom say one negative sentence about the way I was created.

Let me clarify. Mom had no problem making me aware or disciplining me when I was *doing* something wrong. But the way I was created was perfect in every way. If a parent sends the message to a child that the God of the Universe made mistakes when He created her, then how can God become Someone the child can trust?

I've never heard Mom say a negative comment about me to someone else. Sometimes I hear younger mothers say (in front of their children) things like, "Well, Johnny is a slob. He never cleans his room." And so Johnny believes he's a slob. Why? Because his mother said he was.

I once heard a mom say (in her daughter's presence), "Sally doesn't play sports because she is the clumsiest child I've ever seen." Sally's face blushed crimson red with embarrassment. Such statements make me cringe for the kid. Who wants to hear that your own mother is disappointed in the way God made you?

Of course, I'd be lying if I said I never discovered things about myself I didn't like. When I was a teenager and complained to Mom about having a bump on my nose, Mom said the shape of it was an indication that I had "a Roman nose." The way she said the words, "You have a Roman nose, Marie," made me believe that having a Roman nose (whatever that might be) is enviable. I didn't know any Romans, but I believed that if I ever ran into one on the streets of New York, we would both recognize the greatness of our noses.

Years ago, I knew a younger couple whose son was perfectly healthy, but slim and not very tall. His parents wanted a tall, athletic star of a child. And so, when he was eight years old, they took him to a doctor who, for years, injected the boy with Human Growth Hormones in an effort to spur his growth.[7]

What his parents never knew is that the boy would regularly ask the children's minister of his church to pray for him because he was distraught because he was disappointing his parents by not being taller. How can such a child learn to believe that God does all things well when his parents send the message that He didn't when He created that child? Mom's words about me and actions toward me always sent me the message that I was perfect exactly the way God created me.

So let's review:

Molly's Meatball Lesson #1

Honoring God means accepting yourself the way God created you. It also means accepting your children the way God created them and teaching your children to accept how God created them.

Every Meatball Makes Mistakes

"My dear children, I write this to you so that you will not sin. But if anybody does sin, we have an advocate with the Father."

— 1 JOHN 2:1

I don't want you to think that Mom raised me to grow up believing I was destined to be the mistake-maker of the universe. I didn't grow up hearing about her low expectations for me. I grew up hearing about her high expectations of God and His promises. As a child, I knew that Jesus was my Holy Hero, forgiving and defending me before God Himself. What a concept! What freedom to create light-hearted living!

When I was in fourth grade, our class was putting on a patriotic play for the entire assembly, about a thousand kids. Parents were invited. At home, I was taking piano lessons, and my piano teacher had given me "America" ("My County 'Tis of Thee") to learn by memory. The day before the assembly, I played the song through for the first time without looking at the music.

As we were getting ready to leave our classroom to go to the assembly hall, I told my teacher I could play "America" by heart. She said, "Marie, are you sure?" I assured her I could. She changed the entire program and made me the opening act.

A few minutes later, I sat my little body on a long bench in front of a huge baby grand piano. Every student in the school and every parent, including my mother, focused their attention on me. But in the spotlight, I could only remember the first few bars of the song. I played that bar once. Twice. And then I removed my little body from that long bench in front of that huge piano and left the stage.

I was mortified.

After the program, I cried when I saw Mom. She hugged me and said, "Marie, at least you weren't afraid to try." And that was that. If Mom was embarrassed by her overzealous little girl, I never knew it.

Mom used to remind me, "We aren't sinners because we have sinned; we've sinned because we are sinners." In our natural state, we are fallen, but we don't become despondent when we fail because we have an advocate with God Himself, Jesus Christ.

The dictionary defines the word *advocate* with words like "supporter, backer, believer, activist, campaigner, and sponsor." This type of advocacy is what Jesus is doing for you and me in heaven right this minute.

Are you disappointed in yourself as a mom? Tell it to Jesus. Have you made mistakes as a wife? Tell it to Jesus. Don't really feel all that victorious as a Christian? Tell it to Jesus. That's what Mom taught me. You will not be a perfect person, Christian, wife, mother, daughter, friend or any other thing that starts with the word *perfect*. That's why Jesus came. Isn't that the core of Christianity? (Answer: Yes, it is.)

Molly's Meatball Lesson #2

Jesus is your advocate supporter who is in heaven right now,
pleading your
case before God Himself. So lighten up about the mistake thing.

Out of the Frying Pan and into Forgiveness

During my childhood, forgiveness was a process as easy as breathing. And it wasn't restricted to just my brother and me. Mom never hesitated to admit a mistake and to ask her kids to forgive her for it. Neither did Dad. When a kid grows up with parents willing to admit mistakes and then ask their kids for forgiveness, it's a no-brainer that those children will learn not to fear failure.

Don't run from mistakes — because when you look back at your life, you'll discover they were your greatest teachers. My mother's example of how to deal with mistakes is something you may want to consider. Her wisdom goes like this:

- **God Is not surprised by mistakes.** Hiding from God because you've made a mistake is a bigger mistake than the mistake that is causing you to hide from Him. *"As a father has compassion on his children, so the LORD has compassion on those who fear him; for he knows how we are formed, he remembers that we are dust"* (Ps.103:13-14).

- **Admit a mistake at the first possible moment.** In our home, being unwilling to own up to a mistake was unacceptable behavior. I grew up knowing that God knew my heart. He saw everything I did and thought. Even when Mom wasn't around, I knew God was — 24/7. I learned to admit my mistakes, and they were forgiven. It's our prideful reluctance to simply admit it when we're wrong or have made a mistake that opens the door to tormenting guilt. *"Oh Lord, you have examined my heart and know everything about me"* (Ps. 139:1).

- **Ask for forgiveness.** Admitting to a mistake was just the first step toward healing it. Mom taught me to ask the Lord for forgiveness using spoken words. I lived with a sense that God was involved in every aspect of my life. If I needed forgiveness for anything, in any area, I should first ask God. The genius in this is that once a little girl (or a grown woman) has spoken to God about a mistake and His mercy and forgiveness flood her heart, then verbally asking a mere human for forgiveness is a piece of cake. And forgiving others – after you have been so mercifully forgiven – follows closely after. *"Have mercy on me, O God, because of your unfailing love...Against you, and you alone, have I sinned"* (Ps. 51:1, 4, NLT).

- **Fuggheddabboudit (forget about it).** The only thing worse than not admitting a mistake is: admitting it, being forgiven for it, asking others to forgive you for it, and <u>then continuing to feel guilty about it</u>. Just like the piano mishap in the fourth grade, Mom never reminded me of any mistake after I'd admitted it and asked for forgiveness. And neither does God. *"If you, LORD, kept a record of sins, Lord, who could stand? But with you there is forgiveness, so that we can, with reverence, serve you"* (Ps. 130:3-4).

Molly's Meatball Lesson #3

When you make a mistake, admit it. Seek forgiveness for it. Forgive others the way you've been forgiven. And then "fuggheddabboudit."

More Than Qualified

> *"Such confidence we have through Christ before God.*
> *Not that we are competent in ourselves to claim*
> *anything for ourselves,*
> *but our competence comes from God."*

— 2 CORINTHIANS 3:4-5

Mom's confidence in God's faithfulness became part of my DNA from an early age. She modeled a life where it was a greater crime to forget that "through Christ" I was more than qualified to do whatever He (or anyone else) asked me to do. She didn't teach me to think more of myself than I ought to, but to believe that I could try for things that seemed unattainable in my own strength because "through Christ I was able to do all things." She encouraged me to carefully consider every opportunity to serve others in the Body of Christ. She would say, "Prayerfully consider everything as the way God is leading you into new growth. Don't always say yes but also, don't always say no because you don't feel qualified. Don't be afraid to try something you feel challenged by. That's how God will expand upon the gifts He has already given you. It isn't you, anyway, but the Holy Spirit working through you."

I've always been confused when other Christians feel unqualified to do something. They shrink back with insecurity and doubt. It isn't conceit to think that "through Christ" I can do all things. It is Truth. It's conceit to think you can do something in your own power that will have spiritual and eternal results. Who is that naturally talented? No one.

Jesus said, *"The Spirit gives life; the flesh counts for nothing"* (Phil. 4:13, NLT). If the goal is to bring life to a dying world (and that is our primary goal as believers in Christ) we cannot do it in our own strength. If God's pattern is to infuse weak jars of clay with His power so that when something amazing happens, He gets the glory, then no one can use not being qualified as an excuse for inactivity.

Because my mom encouraged me to say yes to whatever God led me to do, I've had wonderful experiences in my life. For five years, I was the hostess of my own television show for women. I'm a songwriter and singer. I've had the honor of hearing Christian artists record the songs I've written. I speak on a regular basis at women's retreats. I've written hundreds of magazine articles. I write two monthly columns for a magazine. I wrote a curriculum for one of the largest denominations on earth to use in their small groups throughout the world.

My point is not to boast but to confess that I had no credentials, no formal training, to do any of those things. But don't tell the people who sing my songs, or read my articles, or listen to me speak at women's events. As a matter of fact, Chapter One of this book may not be the right moment to admit this to you, but I don't know how to write a book. However, the Holy Spirit does. He used regular people to write the Number One best seller of all time. So here I am, Marie Armenia, writing a book with His help. And there you are, reading it. Go figure. Thanks, Mom.

Molly's Meatball Lesson #4

You are more than qualified to do more than you can imagine if you acknowledge that you can only do it through Christ (Phil. 4:13).

2

HOT FLASHES ARE NATURAL BUT GOD IS SUPERNATURAL

The Recipe For Prayer

"Come and hear, all you who fear God; let me tell you what he has done for me.
I cried out to him with my mouth; his praise was on my tongue."

— PSALM 66:16-17

It's the same scenario played over and over for most of my adult life. The phone rings. I answer it. It's someone I know. After some brief and perfunctory "Hello, how are you?" sentences, the individual gets straight to the purpose of their call: Some details of an impossible situation are shared and followed by the question, "Would you ask your mother to pray?" They share some details of an impossible situation they are facing. How cool is it to have a mother whose claim-to-fame is her prayer life? Very cool.

Someone who made such a call was Rita.[8] She was married later in life and desperately wanted to have children of her own. For five years, once a month she would break down in desperation and despair as she realized that once again, she was not pregnant. Anyone who suffers from infertility can attest to the hopelessness of wanting a child and not being able to have one. Finally and as a last resort, sweet Rita, who doubted the existence of God, called me to ask me to ask my mom to pray. I called her back to let her know that my mother said she would "definitely pray." And, yes, the very next month – the very next month – after years of trying, Rita was pregnant. She called me again to announce this good news, but this time she was laughing and screaming and crying all at the same time. She was astounded by the power of prayer. As we spoke about God's incredible mercy and love, I mentioned to Rita that God's love was revealed through the life of another baby 2,000 years ago – His Only Son, Jesus. Realizing what a gift her baby was, she could more easily understand the amazing love it took for God to give His Only Son away as a gift to the world. God, in His mercy, opened her eyes to understand that Jesus came to give Rita life that would last after this life is over. She chose to accept the forgiveness God offers through the cross. She became a new creation while God was creating her baby inside her. Months later, she had a beautiful little girl. Three months after her daughter was born, Rita was happily surprised to learn she was expecting again. She'd have two children born within eleven months of one another. She called me with the good news and then right before hanging up the phone she added, "Oh, by the way, will you ask your mother to *stop* praying?"

Molly's Meatball Lesson #5

Don't be afraid to ask God to do whatever you want Him to do as long as you are willing to accept whatever He decides to do.

This kind of thing has happened over and over and over and over again. I've seen God answer prayers in countless and seemingly impossible situations. I am not sure I can find the words that will convey the incredible power of my mother's prayers and more importantly, the deep, deep love that compels her to pray them. She has lived a lifetime of believing she can boldly approach the very throne of God *"with confidence, so that we may receive mercy and find grace to help us in our time of need"* (Heb.

4:16). So often we may offhandedly tell someone, "I'll pray for you" but we soon forget the urgency of that person's need.

There is something familiar to me when I read the prayer of Jesus in the Gospel of John, Chapter 17. It's because His prayer reminds me of my mother's prayers. The way Jesus speaks to His Father makes it obvious that they have a relationship that comes close to being one. Sounds like my mother. Jesus' first sentences that knowing *"the only true God and Jesus Christ, who you have sent"* is His primary purpose in being alive. Yes, that's my mom, too. She wants others to know that eternal life is found in Jesus and that they can have a real and close relationship with their heavenly Father. Jesus' prayer was one sentence after another of concern and love for God and others. He asks for His followers to be protected, and to be made holy. Yes, just like mom's prayers. He wants them all to be with Him where He is. He says, *"I have made you known to them, and will continue to make you known in order that the love you have for me may be in them and that I myself may be in them"* (John 17:26). Yes, this prayer that Jesus prayed sounds like all the prayers I heard coming from my mother's (and father's) mouth as I was growing up and until this very moment. She loves God. She loves others. I believe that's a primary reason for the power in her prayers. She cares about the people she prays for.

Molly's Meatball Lesson #6

Prayer must have its basis in love. Love for the one you are praying for.
Love for the One you are praying to.

God Is An Equal Opportunity Prayer Answerer

"I call to you, Lord, come quickly to me; hear me when I call to you. May my prayer be set before you like incense; may the lifting up of my hands be like the evening sacrifice."

— Psalm 141:1-2

All through the writing of this book, the thought that I am writing it because I think there is something better about my Mom's walk with the Lord is something I want to avoid. There is no purpose to point to Molly Bruno, unless in pointing to her, someone decides to focus on Jesus. The last thing my mother or I would want is for anyone to walk away from this book thinking, "Wow, God answers Molly Bruno's prayers. He must love her more than He loves me." That isn't the truth or even close to the truth. God wants to hear and answer YOUR prayers too. God is an equal opportunity prayer answerer. My hope is that you might read this book and say something closer to, "Wow, If God answers prayers the way He answers prayers for Molly Bruno, then I know that God will answer my prayers the same way."

However, it would be disingenuous for me to deny that for some reason God answers a lot of her prayers. Here are some things I have learned from her example and I pray they will be an example to you as well:

- **More Attempts At The Plate.**

Pray continually.

— 1 THESSALONIANS 5:17

Her prayer batting average is higher because she has more attempts at the plate. For Mom, every situation, no matter how big or how small has a two-word solution – "Let's pray." Please read what I wrote. In every situation her go-to response is ALWAYS, "Let's pray." Everything is a matter of prayer, every single thing. Simply put, she doesn't try to fit prayer into her life; she fits her life into prayer. She doesn't have a "prayer life." Her life is prayer. Why? She's crazy about God. She WANTS to pray. She WANTS to talk to Him. She WANTS to listen to Him. After decades of praying, she still seeks Him and still wants to know Him more.

She is always talking to God as she walks through her day; however, she also takes the time to separate herself from the world a few times a day to be alone with God. Sounds a lot like Jesus, doesn't it? Someone once said to me that they wish they had my mother's self-discipline toward prayer. I answered them by reflecting that her prayer life does not have its basis in self-discipline any more than you would label it self-discipline when you see a three-year old devouring a bag of his favorite candy. Self-discipline is when you MAKE yourself do something you know you should do. Prayer is like eating candy to my mother - a sweet JOY to her.

Molly's Meatball Lesson #7

The primary purpose of prayer is telling Someone who loves you more than anything that you love Him the same way.

• "Self-Conscious Prayer" Is An Oxymoron

My mother didn't teach me how to pray any more than she taught me how to breathe. I saw her pray REAL prayers, using REAL words addressed to a REAL God. I learned by observing my mother's prayer life that the last thing on earth that should be edited is a prayer. She taught me by example that when a person speaks to God, that person should remember they are speaking to the One who created Truth. He already knows every thought you have. Tell Him whatever is really inside. Speak to Him the way you would speak to anyone. Be real with God because God is real. Editing a prayer to the One who sees your heart is ridiculous. To be afraid to tell the One who made you what's really inside your heart is pointless. Why would someone do that? It baffles my mother. And I believe it baffles God.

Molly's Meatball Lesson #8

A fake prayer is a waste of your time and God's.

• Faith in His Faithfulness

"But without faith it is impossible to please him: for he that cometh
to God must believe that he is, and that he is a rewarder of them
that diligently seek him."

— Hebrews 11:6, KJV

My mother has great faith – but not in her own faith. My mother has great faith in God's faithfulness. She never taught me that if I had enough faith, or the right kind of faith, or the right words of faith, God would be required to answer every prayer I prayed. God does not owe anyone anything. She taught me to have faith in God's faithfulness and His love and in the promises in His Word.

That verse above is one of her favorites, and it's a key to understanding her prayer life. First of all she believes God IS Who He says He is. She believes with a pure and childlike faith whatever the Bible says about God – Who He is, what He does, and what He is going to do. She believes He is Who HE says He is. And more importantly, she knows the Word enough to know exactly WHO He says He is and WHAT He has promised for those who love Him.

So if my mother needs something, she believes He is her Provider. If she is ill, she believes He is her Healer. If she is brokenhearted, she believes He is the God of All Comfort. Her faith is in who GOD IS. She lives her life with the attitude of heart that says, *"God is not a man, that he should lie; neither the son of man, that he should repent: hath he said, and shall he not do it? or hath he spoken, and shall he not make it good?"* (Num. 28:19, KJV).

What I've observed in her is not something I've observed in many people. I've seen people who fall apart when life gets difficult. To be honest, I have had moments of falling apart when life gets difficult. But my mom has spent her life devoted to knowing God – through prayer and through His Word – and she knows that He will never send anything her way that isn't born out of His love for her. She doesn't simply know the Word. She knows the One who wrote it.

Hebrews 11:6 also says that God rewards people. What kind of people? People who are "diligently seeking." Diligently seeking what? Answers to prayers? No. Diligently seeking Him. He rewards those people whose primary purpose in prayer is to seek Him. Her prayer life is about knowing God more. Hearing God more. That's WHY SHE PRAYS. The fact that He also answers her requests is simply spiritual icing on the cake.

If you know someone who believes they have God all figured out and doesn't need to seek Him any further, I believe you know someone who hardly knows God at all. My mother's reward for diligently seeking the Lord is knowing the Lord in a deep and almost intimate way. And that's reward enough for her. She isn't trying to get answers. She is simply trying to know Him more.

Molly's Meatball Lesson #9

If God alone is not reward enough for you, then nothing else ever will be.

- **Nothing Is Too Small To Pray About**

"Look at the birds of the air; they do not sow or reap or store away in barns, and yet your heavenly Father feed them. Are you not more valuable than they?"

— MATTHEW 7:26

For her last birthday, we bought my mother a bird feeder and a birdbath. Who knew what joy it would bring her to watch the birds in her backyard? I didn't. We bought her a book so she can identify the birds she sees, and she just delights in watching the birds. They fascinate her. My husband decided to add a hummingbird feeder to the scene. He installed it close to her kitchen window and she was as excited as a kid. New York City is not known for being a hotbed of nature, and as such, she had never seen a hummingbird. She and I sat in front of her window for a few minutes.

I told her it would take a few days, maybe weeks, until a hummingbird discovered this new feeder. I explained how they would arrive and hover over the feeder, and stick their long beaks into each hole. She wanted to see a hummingbird and she wanted to see one right away. I re-explained it would take a while for them to discover this feeder because they are creatures of habit and probably already had some feeders they were using. A while? Really? She prayed out loud in front of my husband and me, "Lord, would you send a hummingbird to this feeder so I can see one?" My husband is my witness that less than ten seconds later a hummingbird appeared right in front of her window. It was lingering there as if God was saying, "Here you go, Molly. You asked for a hummingbird? Here it is. This is what a hummingbird looks like." She held her breath in awe and watched it drink from the bright red hummingbird feeder. For weeks after that she never saw another hummingbird. She believes that first hummingbird was sent as a gift from God. Who's gonna argue with her? Not me. Would I have even thought to bother the God of the Universe and ask Him to send a hummingbird to a hummingbird feeder in the backyard of my house? No, I would not. All I know is that she asked and seconds later there was a hummingbird. I'm reporting. You decide.

Molly's Meatball Lesson #10

Praying to God about your every day cares and needs –
big or small - is the
way your children and others will learn that God cares
about their every
day cares and needs – big or small.

- **Nothing Is Too Big To Pray About**

"You have collected all my tears in your bottle.
You have recorded each one in your book."

— Psalm 56:8, NLT

When I was a little girl, I remember the time my mom was having extreme pain in her lower back. She went to her doctor. After taking some X-rays her doctor informed her that she had huge and dangerous kidney stones. So severe was her situation that he was sending her to the hospital directly from his office. He explained that surgery was necessary. (This was decades ago. Before the medical advances we take for granted now). He left the room to call the hospital to get her a room. As my mother sat in the cold and lonely examining room, she knew she didn't want to have to go to the hospital, she didn't want to have surgery. A verse came to her mind about God saving our tears in a bottle.[9]

As she sat there, she whispered a prayer, saying, "Lord, I'm sitting in a doctor's exam room. It isn't the place for me to cry out to you in desperation and ask You to deliver me and heal me. But Lord, do You remember all those times I simply sat at your feet and didn't ask You for a thing? I just worshiped You with tears of thankfulness and love? You bottled those tears, didn't You? Would You take some of those tears, Lord, and apply them to this situation? Would You heal these kidney stones? Would You take away this pain?"

Her doctor returned with the news that the hospital was waiting for her, and he was going to take a second set of X-rays for her to take with her. This was long before the age of computers and sending files through emails. A few moments later, the doctor returned with a perplexed look on his face. He held up the first set of X-rays and said "Mrs. Bruno, on this first set of X-rays, do you see the stones there, in your kidney?" He pointed to an area and my mother could see something there. She nodded yes. He continued, "Now, Mrs. Bruno here are the X-rays I just took. Do you see the stones there anymore?" Whatever was in the first X-ray was not in the second one, or the subsequent third X-ray he took to confirm what he saw in the second one. He came back in, "Mrs. Bruno, the kidney stones have disappeared."

"Now that you mention it, Doctor, so has my pain."

She got up, got dressed and my father drove her home. From that that day to this day, she has never had a problem with her kidneys again.

Molly's Meatball Lesson #11

Don't teach your children to expect God to perform a
miracle every day,
but don't forget to let them know when He does.

Hot Flashes are Natural but God is Supernatural

"Woman, you have great faith! Your request is granted."

— MATTHEW 15:28

It happened on a Sunday morning, my mother's favorite day of the week. On the Sunday morning this happened, I'm sure she was dressed impeccably in a three-piece "pastor's wife" kind of suit, with a matching blouse, and stylish heels with a matching purse. She always dresses with style. My mother is beautiful on the inside, but she is also a beautiful woman on the outside. Even at her age, she has beautiful wrinkle-free skin, almost fluorescent colored green eyes and a glow that radiates from the inside out. I also feel confident that on the Sunday morning in question, her hair was fixed and sprayed into a layered and bubbly coif without one hair out of place. I know she was wearing a matching pin on the lapel of her suit jacket. She loves pins.

Anyway, my father had just ended the morning worship service, and the church members were milling around in the lobby. After each church service she was always surrounded by "Her Girls," which is what she called the group of women in our church. The lobby would be filled with the sounds of loud and happy chattering as the women she mentored gathered around Momma Molly to hear her stories, or to tell her one. It was love in the church lobby.

It was during one of these happy fellowship moments that suddenly and without warning something happened that almost stopped The Unstoppable Molly Bruno dead in her tracks. She recalls, "All of sudden, from out of nowhere, came a wave of heat that started at the base of my spine and worked its way up my back and down my arms. It went up my scalp and down my face. I was instantly engulfed in a consuming wave of heat that made me feel flushed and feverish. I thought I was dying. And then, as quickly as it came, it went away." She was shaken by what had just happened to her. On the drive home from church, I remember her telling my father about it. He just kind of nodded a "I don't know what that was" nod. When she got home from church, she called each of her four sisters to report the event. They matter-of-factly said, "Oh, don't worry about it. You just had your first hot flash. You'll keep having them now for a couple of years. There's nothing you can do. It's natural.'"

My mother's generation is the first generation to actually live long enough to come out the other side of menopause. The life expectancy for women living in the United States 100 years ago was 52 years of age.[10] When this was happening to my mom 40 years ago, there wasn't a lot of information about hot flashes or the Menopause Monster.

It's true that menopause is a natural season but so are cicada harvests. They are both annoying. Most women do our best to endure menopause without doing anything that might cause us to serve jail time. Eventually with the help of God we outlive the season. Who would have the audacity and boldness to ask God to change her change? My mother, that's who.

I remember the prayer she prayed that Sunday afternoon, "Lord, they tell me these are hot flashes. If having hot flashes is something You want for me because it's natural and Your will, then I accept them. Lord, they may be natural but You are supernatural. I'm asking that I never have another hot flash as long as I live." And she never did. Honest. She never did.

"With man this is impossible, but not with God; all things are possible with God."

— MARK 10:27

Molly's Meatball Lesson #12

Let your children see and hear you asking God for what seems impossible. It's the only way they will learn for themselves that with God nothing is impossible.

Doesn't Everybody Put Their Bills On Top Of The Refrigerator?

"Therefore do not worry about tomorrow, for tomorrow will worry about itself."

— MATTHEW 6:34

When I was about ten years old, I overheard my mother praying out loud in the kitchen after I returned home from school one day. Evidently, there was an unexpected expense for $500. She was talking to God and telling Him, "Lord, You already know that we don't have the money to pay this $500 and You know it's due tomorrow. I don't know where to get this money. I have been worried all day about this. But now, I am giving this problem to You, Father. Please help us." And with that, I saw her take the bill papers and place them on top of the refrigerator like it was a holy altar. My parents were hard workers and good stewards of their money. We weren't rich by any means, but it was unusual for something to come along that would cause them to be so financially strapped. I don't know the details. I was just a kid. I just heard the prayer. I just saw her cast her cares upon the Lord. I saw her trusting that He cared for her. (See 1 Pet. 5:7.)

The rest of the afternoon she was perfectly fine. If I hadn't overheard her prayer, I would never have known anything was wrong. When my dad got home from work at about 5:30, she said to him, "Your father called ten minutes ago. He asked if you could go there as soon as you got home from work." My grandparents lived nearby, and my father often went there in the evenings to check on them. We all just assumed Grandpa needed help with something. My dad left for my grandparents' house before he could even take off his coat.

About 30 minutes later, he walked back in the house and said, "My father said that a few hours ago, he felt a strong urge to give me $500. He felt it was important for me to have it before tomorrow." My grandparents didn't hand out $500 on a regular basis. I was setting the table for dinner and his sentence took my breath away. My mother hadn't had the time to tell my father that the family's bills were on top of the refrigerator and that she was worried. My grandfather, for sure, could not have known. No one but God, my mother, and I knew that she had placed the situation completely in His hands. One thing I knew: I was seeing a miracle right before my ten-year-old eyes. However, on that day, a mere two hours after hearing my mother pray a desperate prayer, a ten year old girl learned a great big lesson about God: He's real, He answers prayer, He cares about your needs, and if you put your bills on top of the refrigerator, He will give you the money to pay them. (Only kidding about the refrigerator part.)

Molly's Meatball Lesson #13

*If God is a real and living and ever present help in times of trouble in **your** everyday life, He will be a real and living and ever present help in times of*
trouble in the everyday lives of your children, your family, your neighbors
and everyone who knows you.

Sometimes, Worrying Is The Right Thing to Do, Right?

"Can any one of you by worrying add a single hour to your life?"

— MATTHEW 6:27

Fast-forward a few decades and I am in New York City in September to help my parents with last-minute packing. They have decided to sell the house my brother and I grew up in and move near Nashville to be with us and our spouses, children and grandchildren. Without trying, our whole family had settled in Tennessee over the last few years. So when my father retired as a pastor, it was natural that my aging parents would move from New York City to Music City to be closer to their entire family. Our family had a well thought-out "Plan To Move Our Parents." The closing on their house was Monday, September 17.

I was flying by myself on Friday, September 7, to help them. I would finish up with all the packing and I would fly home on Wednesday, September 12. My husband and brother would fly to New York City on Sunday, September 16. They'd pick up the rental truck we had reserved and pack the truck. On Monday, September 17, they would drive my parents to the attorney's office for the closing, then drive them to the airport to fly to Tennessee. The two of them would drive the rental truck and my parents' car to Nashville, arriving a day or two later, and we would all live happily ever after as New York Yankees in the heart of Dixie.

I mention all these insignificant dates because right in the middle of them all, a most significant date in the history of our country occurred. On September 11, 2001, some evil people obliterated The World Trade Center and the lives of 3,000 innocent people. Everything stopped as stoic New Yorkers stood together in horrible, grim-faced grief. September 11, 2001. I was there. I remember how clear and blue the sky was that morning. I was reading the Bible on the back porch. I was looking forward to getting back to Tennessee the next day as I anxiously awaited the birth of my first grandchild. Life was good. And then life was horrifying. Communication in New York City was virtually impossible as phones, and computers, and cable news were all disrupted.

We forgot about houses, moving, closings and planes. Our thoughts were on the people who were grieving the people they knew and loved who had simply gone to work one day and never came home. We didn't know if the young couple who had purchased the house had even survived. We knew they both worked in Lower Manhattan. Honestly? Selling the house, closing on the house, anything about the house was the last thing we cared about.

However, two days later, on Thursday the phone service was finally working pretty regularly. The buyer's attorney called to inform us that his clients were still anxious to move into their home the following Monday. Thankfully, they had survived the attack. I said, "Sure, right, OK."

It was surreal to know scores of people who had lost their lives in one moment on a Tuesday morning and here two days later, life still had to go on. I had to figure out a way to get my parents moved out of their house the following Monday. My brain started working on "Plan B To Move Our Parents." I wasn't very successful at formulating it.

On Friday morning, my parents and I sat around the kitchen table. My husband had decided to drive to New York from Nashville. I'd just called the truck rental place to see if there was any chance we could still have a rental truck on Sunday. The owner snapped, "Lady! Gimme a break! You think you can just rent an empty truck anywhere within 300 miles of New York City? You're kidding me, right?" And he hung up on me. At that very moment, my husband walked through the door.

All he had to do was look at me and see I was in a panic. A truly weak and unspiritual one. I figured it was OK to panic. We were in a terrorist attack mindset. I explained our dilemma to him, "We have to move them out by Monday. But how? What do we do? What do we do?" Yes, I kept repeating that. My mother heard me explaining and saw my panic. She suggested her go-to solution in every situation, saying, "Let's pray."

Can I be honest? I wanted to say, "Really, Mom? Really? I know that you want to pray, but really, Mom, prayer is not going to work this time. God understands that we need to figure this out. THIS IS A NATIONAL DISASTER, MOM!! Sometimes, Mom, even God understands that worrying is the right thing to do."

Of course, my mother didn't raise a fool. I didn't say a word, and I closed my eyes as she prayed the simplest, childlike of prayers. "Lord, You see our situation. This is no surprise to You. Lord, please help us. We need to find a way to move our stuff. Thank you, Lord. Amen." And with that she turned to offer Phil a bagel.

I know that God sees the heart, but really, in the history of prayers, it was not a National Emergency kind of prayer. It was a brief four-sentence prayer in a situation that I felt required a few paragraphs with a raised voice explanation to God. I felt we needed more emotion. I felt her prayer should have been prayed at a high level, high volume emotional explanatory type prayer. Something like, "GOD!!!! HELP US!!!! HELP US GOD! WE JUST HAD A TERRORIST ATTACK. I hate to bother

You with something so small and insignificant in light of what just happened, but THERE ARE NO MOVING TRUCKS AVAILABLE TO MOVE US!" I felt we needed more panic. More emotion. More hysteria. More desperation. Nope. Just a quiet and calm, "Lord, you're aware we need help, right? We know You will help us." And then she's making bagels for people? I thought, "A bagel? You're making a bagel, Mom? Phil, you're eating a bagel? Really? Does anyone see the situation we are currently in?"

I assumed I was the only one who was aware enough to comprehend that the whole world had changed in an instant. We needed to figure this out. And we needed to figure it out right now! I wasn't counting on that prayer to get us any help, I'll tell you that.

And then it happened. A mere three (possibly as little as two) minutes later, the wall phone rang. Since I was the one standing close enough to the wall to bang my head against it, I was the one who answered it. There was a woman on the other end and she said, "Hello. This is Stephenson's Moving Company. Does anyone there need a moving truck?"

I almost dropped the phone. My parents and Phil, were sitting at the table noshing their bagels and didn't know what the woman had said to me. In disbelief I asked the woman, "Are you really a moving company calling us to ask us if we need a moving truck." They were. I realized that it was another miraculous answer to another prayer my mother had prayed. It was like seeing the Red Sea parting.

The estimator was there in less than an hour, walking through the house. We called my parents' attorney and he arranged for my parents to sign the necessary closing papers on Friday afternoon. At 3:00 PM on Saturday, less than 24 hours from my panic and worrying episode in the kitchen, and less than 24 hours after my mother prayed the simplest prayer of faith, we saw the moving truck filled with their life's possessions drive away. It was Plan C to move our parents: "Call on the Lord." I learned that day that a terrorist attack changes everything but the faithfulness of God.

Molly's Meatball Lesson #14

Don't start shaking when the world starts shaking.
Heaven never has a
national emergency. And prayer is always the only solution.

"Mema Prayed For Me"

My mother loves her children, her grandchildren, and great-grandchildren. Our family knows that her prayers have been the reason why God has turned so many situations around in our family. It's another book on another day to tell of the miracles and mercy of God on our family.

One answer to prayer stands out. When my son was in kindergarten, we noticed his eyes turning in as he wrote. A trip to a pediatric eye specialist at Johns Hopkins in Baltimore confirmed that the muscles in his eyes were causing him to turn his eyes in. As a result, he was required to wear very thick glasses.

Now, my mother has nothing against glasses or the people who wear them. As a matter of fact, my father has worn glasses since the day she met him. But for some reason, she decided, "I'm going to pray that God heals Philip's eyes." I thought, "Enjoy yourself, Mom. He will have to wear them for at least the next decade, according to the specialist." I simply said, "OK" and forgot about it. A few weeks later, my son came down for breakfast before school. He put his glasses on. The same glasses he had worn the day before. The glasses he had been wearing every day for months. He said, "Mom, I can't see out of my glasses." I cleaned them. He put them back on. "No, Mom, everything is blurry. I see better without them." He took his glasses off that morning and never put them on again. A trip to the eye specialist confirmed that, in his words, "our course of treatment seems to have corrected the muscle problem in your son's eyes sooner than expected." And that was the first time my own son began to see that nothing is impossible with God. And how good it is to have a praying grandmother. My prayer is that someday, my grandchildren, who also call me "Mema" will be able to remember a time in their lives where God did something amazing and impossible because "Mema prayed."

Molly's Meatball Lesson #15

Your children will learn to pray from the prayers they hear
at home more
than the prayers they hear at church.

The Shameless Audacity of Persistent Prayer

My life with my mother reminds me of the day the disciples asked Jesus, "Lord, teach us to pray." They approached Jesus because they *observed Him praying. "Jesus was praying in a certain place"* (Luke 11:1). My mother didn't TEACH me to pray; I SAW her praying. A mom who prays in front of her children will have children who want to learn how to pray.

The disciples saw Jesus praying and that's why they wanted to learn how to pray. I saw my mother praying and that's why I wanted to learn how to pray. In response to their request, Jesus gave us all what we call "The Lord's Prayer" (Luke 11:2-4) as an example of how to pray. But He further explained prayer to them in the verses immediately following (Luke 11:5-8). He told the disciples a story in which they were the lead characters. He asked them to imagine themselves knocking on a neighbor's door at midnight to borrow bread to feed a friend who has arrived unexpectedly. Jesus explained, *"I tell you, even though he will not get up and give you the bread because of friendship, yet because of your shameless audacity he will surely get up and give you as much as you need."*

Shameless audacity. Those words remind me of my mother's approach to prayer. She has no fear of God's displeasure or that He might scold her for asking for impossible things. She has no need to edit her heart to the One she loves. She knows He knows her heart. Having settled this between herself and God, she asks. And asks again. As Jesus taught in that same session with the disciples, *"I say to you: Ask and it will be given to you; seek and you will find; knock and the door will be opened to you. For everyone who asks receives; the one who seeks finds; and to the one who knocks, the door will be opened"* (Luke 11:9-10).

And just like the person in the parable of Jesus, her prayers are usually not for herself but for the needs of others. She's asking her Friend to help her friends. And she kept and keeps the situation between friends – the One in Heaven and the one on earth. Through my growing up years, when someone called to ask for prayer or when they pulled her aside after church to speak to her, she never divulged what she was praying about. I love that Mom never let me know one thing about the people she prayed for. I just knew she was praying about something urgent.

Molly's Meatball Lesson #16

If prayer is your first response in every situation, it will become your children's first response in every situation.

But most of all, when I think of my mother's prayers, I remember the prayer she prayed every morning without fail, "Lord, please send someone my way today that I can tell about You." For Mom, the greatest thing about being alive is for God to give her the honor of leading someone from death into life. So she asks Him to send people her way. And every day, He does. She is a "Wonder of A Witnessing Woman."

3

IT'S NOT BY CHANCE YOU CALLED HERE

The Recipe For Witnessing

"But how can they call on him to save them unless they believe in him? And how can they believe in him if they have never heard about him? And how can they hear about him unless someone tells them?"

— ROMANS 10:14, NLT

New York City is a collection of five boroughs. I grew up in Staten Island, which got its name because a Dutch guy visited the place in 1609 and thought it would be cool to name it after the Dutch parliament — *Staaten Eylandt.*[11]   Really? That would be similar to discovering a new planet and naming it *Congress.*

Anyway, because it's an island, Staten Islanders have to use a bridge to get to any of the other boroughs. (Unless they choose to use the Staten Island Ferry to get to Manhattan, the other island which is one of the boroughs.)

The Outerbridge Crossing[12] is one of four bridges on Staten Island. It connects to New Jersey and was named after a man named Eugenius Harvey

Outerbridge. I love that this guy's parents named him You Genius; however, many Staten Islanders are perplexed as to why someone decided to name a bridge after a man whose name ends with the word *bridge*, as if life is not difficult enough in New York City. Anyway, Staten Islanders simply call it the Outer Bridge, as if it was named after someone with the last name Outer. It was built in 1928, and more than 90,000 cars travel over it every day.

It was over this old and busy structure that my parents were traveling one day when they witnessed a tragic event. A man stopped his car in the middle of the bridge, ran to the side of the structure, and jumped. The Outer Bridge is 135 feet above the water, which is more than high enough to kill someone who wants to die.[13] All traffic came to a screeching halt. In a matter of moments, there were hundreds of people standing on the side of the bridge, looking for the jumper.

My mother saw him first. He survived the fall and was swimming to grab one of the concrete columns holding up the bridge. Mom's only thought was that the man could die any minute, and he needed to hear about Jesus. The fact that she was standing on top of the bridge and he was struggling to stay alive in the water 135 feet below her were not witnessing deterrents. FYI: Nothing is a witnessing deterrent to Molly Bruno.

Mom cupped her hands and cried with the loudest voice she could muster, "JESUS LOVES YOU!" Her cry immediately silenced the crowd, and my mom became more fascinating to them than the man struggling to stay alive in the water under the bridge.

Unbelievably, from the dark and dirty New York City waters below the bridge, a voice rose from the water, "I NEED JESUS! WILL HE HELP ME?"

My mother cupped her hands again, "YES! JESUS WILL HELP YOU!"

From the water, "I HAVE DONE TERRIBLE THINGS. WILL JESUS FORGIVE ME?"

From the bridge, "YES! CALL OUT TO HIM RIGHT WHERE YOU ARE. PRAY AND ASK HIM TO FORGIVE YOU OF ALL OF YOUR SIN!"

From the water, "HE WILL FORGIVE ME? ARE YOU SURE?"

From the bridge, "YES! I'M SURE!"

And from 135 feet above him, my mother heard this man crying out to God for mercy and forgiveness. And right there in that water, he was given a new, clean, pure white heart. He became a new creature in Christ. Eventually, the police arrived to rescue him. My mother went her way rejoicing that someone had not entered eternity separated from God.

The next day, the local newspaper reported the story of a man who had attempted suicide by jumping off the Outer Bridge because he had killed his wife and her boyfriend.

God forgave that man. The State of New York, however, did not. He is now serving a life sentence. My mother asked some men from a local prison ministry to visit him and give him a Bible. The last we heard, he was leading others to know the same Jesus who had rescued him.

Nothing is a witnessing deterrent to my mother. No one is too far gone, no one is too religious, and no one is too angry or rebellious enough to keep her from speaking the greatest truth ever known to humanity: Jesus loves you. If you are someone who is sure that God is angry at you for something you have done, then hear this truth: Jesus loves you. No mistake you have made, no sin you have committed, and no vulgar act or selfish behavior will ever change the utter, holy truth: Jesus loves you. Just the way you are as you read these words. Just. The. Way. You. Are.

And if you are someone who believes that anyone you know is beyond you telling them ONE MORE TIME that Jesus loves them, I pray these words have changed your heart and will open your mouth to tell someone you know, "Jesus loves you." Because, He does.

Molly's Meatball Lesson #17

Where there's a will, there's a witness. It's always God's will for you to witness about Jesus.

The Most Important Thing

Telling someone about Jesus is the primary goal of my mother's life. The way she sees it, rescuing someone from eternal hell trumps any other thing you can do with your time here on planet earth. As I mentioned at the end of the last chapter, when I was growing up and until this very day, she prays the same prayer every day: "Lord, please send someone across my path today that I can talk to about You."

And He does.

Nothing is an obstacle to Mom, and everyone is her mission field. These days, at 92, she doesn't get out as much as she used to, but she prays with the man who mows her lawn, witnesses to the UPS guy who delivers her packages, and talks about Jesus to every telemarketer who calls to sell her something. She'll say, "It's not by chance you called here..." and will then launch into what Jesus has done in her life.

The joy Mom receives from leading someone to a relationship with Christ keeps her young, no matter how old she gets. As long as Molly Bruno has breath in her body, she will be winning souls for Jesus.

Mom often recites this quote: "Only one life, T'will soon be past. Only what's done for Christ will last."

I say it to myself more than she realizes. And I taught it to my only son. And he is teaching it to his children.

Molly's Meatball Lesson #18

If you want your children to focus on the things that matter to God, you have to first focus on the things that matter to God.

Jerusalem First

"But you will receive power when the Holy Spirit comes on you;
and you will be my witnesses in Jerusalem,
and in all Judea and Samaria, and to the ends of the earth."

— Acts 1:8

My mom's lesson to me about being a witness was based on that verse. Mom used to remind me that the first place Jesus mentioned that they would be His witnesses *is where they happened to be at that very moment*. It was her way of reminding me that we have to be devoted to witnessing right where we live and be devoted to it every day we live there. Sure, we can go to the uttermost ends of the earth, but first and foremost we must be His witnesses right where we are at any given moment. Granted, it's great to take mission trips for a week or two, and care about people in faraway places, but Mom's philosophy is that God ALSO loves the people who walk in and out of your everyday life just as much as those who live 9,000 miles away. Her life reflects that attitude. She witnesses to whoever she meets, wherever she meets them.

I call it this perspective Mom's "First in Jerusalem Witnessing Plan." Her life is an example of this. At the season in her life when age keeps her from "going into all the world" to be His witness, God has arranged it so that all the world is coming to her. I mean, aren't you reading this book about her? Isn't it amazing that a 92-year-old woman, without a publicist, or a manager, who has never made any attempt to gain any fame is the woman you are reading about right now? I think it's because she is always focused on her "Jerusalem" – her neighbors, her family. She keeps the witnessing switch on at all times and in all places. Mom is always in "Go!" mode. If you're breathing and within ten feet of Molly Bruno, you will hear the gospel. Oh, yes, you will.

Home Run at Yankee Stadium

My parents love the New York Yankees and they never miss a Yankee game on TV. My mother is familiar with every player on the team and can hold her own discussing the Yankees with my brother, my husband, and all the other baseball fans in the family.

Years ago, a church member offered four tickets to my parents and another pastor on staff and his wife to go to a game at Yankee Stadium. Seeing a game live there was a rare treat for them. We were all thrilled that they were going. My mother enjoys every single thing about being alive and this must have been excitement overload for her. I can imagine her eyes focused on the players. During the game, a woman sitting in their section of the ballpark caught a fly ball with her bare hands. Everyone cheered for her, but the ball jammed her ring into her finger and she was in severe pain. She sat there crying from the pain. The paramedics were summoned to assist her. While the game continued on the field, Mom got up from her seat and went and sat next to that woman and comforted her. After the paramedics had arrived, they cut off her ring, and the pain began to subside. My mother continued to sit there with this total stranger and comfort her. This meant she was giving up this rare opportunity to see the Yankees play, in order to sit next to and comfort someone she didn't know and would never see again.

After the pain had subsided, the woman turned to my mom and asked, "Thank you for being so kind to me. Thank you for caring about my pain. Why did you come up here and stay with me?" Mom answered, "I wanted to help you. And now that you feel better, I want to tell you that Jesus loves you." What? Witness in the middle of a baseball game at Yankee Stadium? Oh, you better believe it. And believe it or not, the woman was very hungry for the food that would feed her soul. While the game was continuing on the field, my mother saw another soul who was passing from death into life. My mother told her what it means to be forgiven. And right there at Yankee stadium, the woman bowed her head, and repented of her sin, and accepted Jesus. My mom walked her down to meet my father and the other pastor and his wife. The woman told them, "I just gave my life to Jesus." Her face was glowing, according to the other pastor's wife. She was connected to a church, and became a follower of Jesus. Molly hit a home run for Jesus at Yankee Stadium because, to her, Yankee Stadium was located in her Jerusalem at the moment.

Molly's Meatball Lesson #19

Everywhere you go is a mission field, your Jerusalem.
Everyone you know is a mission field, especially your own children.

"Hey Lady, Get The @(#*@ Outta Here!"

"This is the verdict: Light has come into the world, but people loved darkness instead of light because their deeds were evil."

— JOHN 3:19

Mom heard the car brakes screeching in the middle of the night on the busy street behind her home. Seconds later the deafening sounds of a car accident. She heard screams and horns blaring. My father was asleep. So of course, she decided to get dressed and run out back to the scene of the accident in the middle of the night. The police officers arrived about the same time Mom did. To her horror, she saw a twenty-something man whose head had crashed through his windshield. He was unconscious. She waited on the side of the road and prayed for him. The paramedics arrived but the young man did not respond to treatment. She was concerned that the driver was dead or dying. She didn't know if he knew Jesus. So she walked through the crowd, past the police and the paramedics and right up to the car. Everyone just kind of backed up, assuming perhaps that this woman had some kind of connection to this man who was severely hurt. She walked up to him where he lay, put her hand on his head and said, "Son, call on Jesus. Call on Jesus! Only Jesus can help you. Only Jesus can help you!" To the amazement of everyone there, the young man started to say the name of Jesus. As he did, his consciousness returned. She kept telling him, "Call on Jesus" and he would weakly respond, "Jesus." Eventually he was fully conscious. He looked up at my mother and said, "Hey lady, get the @(#*@ outta here!" The police, realizing the driver didn't know my mother, asked her to leave the scene. She did. But when she tells this story, she says, "I am still praying for that boy, wherever he is, to come to the knowledge of Jesus and Who He is." The percentage of people who reject my mother's witnessing attempts is much higher than the people who receive it. She doesn't let that deter her.

Molly's Meatball Lesson #20

Just because some people reject the gospel doesn't mean you should stop preaching it.

Clean Up on Aisle Two

A few years ago, I went with Mom to a local grocery (I usually shop at another store in town). When we walked through the door, I was stunned by the reception Mom received from employees. When I walk in a grocery store, maybe someone will nod at me. But when my mom walked in she was greeted with something close to adoration as the checkout clerks, the store manager, and other employees ran to greet her. Several women ran over to hug her. I thought, *What's going on? Is this some kind of hidden camera TV show?*

My mother explained and introduced me, "Marie, this is Rita. She gave her heart to Jesus last month." And Rita ran to get her purse to show me the Bible Mom had given her. One by one, at least seven people explained to me what my mother meant to them.

We then walked over to the bakery department, where Mom introduced me to Henry, the department manager. Henry gave Mom a big hug while telling me, "Your mother told me about Jesus. I'd never heard it the way she explained it." His face was glowing! It's amazing that someone like Henry could live in the United States and claim he had never heard the real gospel — but obviously he never understood it until Mom made it perfectly clear.

Henry continued speaking to Mom, so I took my cart and started shopping. About ten minutes later, I see my mother, out of breath and running toward me down aisle two. I thought something was wrong because of the look of urgency on her face. She says, "Hurry, Marie! I need you to come and speak with the produce manager. He is so hungry for God. Hurry! Come!"

I immediately followed her (a person does not argue with a witnessing Molly Bruno) pushing my cart and trying to keep up with her. I was breathless as I asked, "But Mom, why don't you talk with him?" Her reply? "I was, but then a woman in the deli heard me talking to Henry, and now I'm speaking with her. The produce guy had to go in the back, and when he comes back to the front, I need someone to tell him about Jesus while I tell the lady in the deli department. Hurry! Hurry!"

I spoke to the produce manager about the Lord. He'd been burned by church, but seemed to receive what we discussed. He said he would go home and think about what we'd discussed. It felt different sharing the gospel with someone who was unloading bananas as we spoke but it felt real to me. I knew my mom would take care of following up on him.

And Mom? Well, she led a sweet woman to faith in Jesus as they leaned over ham and salami in the deli department. The woman's tears hit the top of the glass counter, and God was making a new creature right there in my mother's Salami Jerusalem.

I mean, who does this kind of stuff? My mother, that's who. That grocery store is in her Jerusalem.

Molly's Meatball Lesson #21

Almost everyone you meet is someone separated from God.
Remember this. All day. Every day. Everywhere.

When I was growing up, I was Mom's Jerusalem. The only picture of a successful life on earth that she painted for me was to love God and to live for Him. I knew I could do all things through Christ. I knew that her definition of success for me never wavered. Love God. Love His people. The End. Making money? Not important. Making a name? Not important. Making disciples of all men. The only important thing a person could do.

She didn't try to talk me into loving God. She didn't try to Bible-bash me. She just loved Him passionately in front of me. She just read the Bible as if it was a specific letter from God to her. I just watched the love she had for Him. I couldn't deny that God was real because He was so visible in our home. Mom once told me, "Marie, I would rather have you live far away in China, never see you again here on earth, and know you were in God's will than have you live next door to me and be out of God's will." Now that's a powerful statement, one that sticks with a kid. That I belonged to God MORE THAN I belonged to her reminded me of whose I truly was.

Mom didn't come up with this wisdom on her own; it's straight from God, who instructs parents to live a godly example in the home: *"Teach them to your children, talking about them when you sit at home and when you walk along the road, when you lie down and when you get up"* (Deut. 11:19).

That pretty much describes my childhood. It wasn't what Mom and Dad said but how they lived that magnetized me to God. All day, every day, Jesus was the very real and very central figure in our home and in our lives. God and His ways, His Word, His will, and His people were the center of our family's universe. Her life proved to me that if I wanted my son to love God, I had to love Him first. If I wanted my son to hear God's Word, I had to tell him first. If I wanted my son to live a life devoted to God and His purposes, I had to live it first. If I wanted my son to pray about everything, I had to pray about everything.

This is not as easy as simply sending your kid to children's church. This takes a daily and lifelong devotion to your own child that will cost you some free time and cause you to notice how you are living the life in front of the ones you gave life to. Far too many Christian parents today do not make serving the Lord in front of their children the priority at home. You can have the best youth pastor ever invented, but he can never be a replacement for a mom and dad who live at home what they say they believe in church.

I was my mother's Jerusalem and I was and am so thankful I was.

Molly's Meatball Lesson #22

If you want your children to be real in front of God and others,
they need
to see you being real in front of God and others.

No Wrong Numbers

Because my mother specifically prays every day that God will give her the honor of being able to tell someone about Jesus, she sincerely believes that every person who crosses her path is a God-ordained assignment from Heaven. She doesn't want to miss one opportunity to lead someone from death into life, out of the darkness and into the light. So she explains to unsuspecting people, "It's not by chance you are here..." or "It's not by chance you called here."

Before the invention of Caller ID, people used to make obscene and harassing phone calls because they could remain anonymous. When I was growing up, I cannot tell you the times I heard Mom say, "Now, son, it's not by chance you called here. You need Jesus. You know that you shouldn't speak that way. Jesus loves you, son. You need Him. Let me pray with you." The caller would hang up immediately.

One night, the phone rang at 3:00 AM and there was a woman on the other end. The ringing of the phone woke me up and I heard my mom talking to her. The woman asked for a man by name and my mother explained that there was no one there by that name. "You dialed the wrong number. There's no one here by that name." The caller was about to hang up when my mother said, "Miss! Miss! It's not by chance you called here." She then began talking to the caller about the love of God. As it turns out, the woman had been trying to call a local bar. Her husband was there (again) and her intent was to tell him that she was going to kill herself before he got home. She had reached a point of such despair about her marriage and the way her husband was treating her, that she decided that ending her life would end the pain. My mother explained that was the wrong choice. She explained that Jesus loved her. She cried with the woman as the woman spent hours talking to my mom about her life. And then, right there on the phone, after talking with Mom for hours, the woman accepted Christ. From that day forward everything changed about her life. God's love – coming through my loving mother – saved her life. In Mom's world, there are no wrong numbers.

Molly's Meatball Lesson #23

The best way to teach your children to witness is to let them see you doing it.

A Bridge and a Blizzard

As I explained earlier, living on Staten Island means you cross a lot of bridges to get anywhere. The bridge closest to our home is the Verrazano Narrows Bridge. There was some controversy surrounding the name because some people just wanted to name it The Narrows Bridge because it spans the body of water called The Narrows. Other people wanted to name it after Giovanni da Verrazano, who was, supposedly, the first European to sail into New York Harbor in 1524, though there are no eyewitnesses to the event. My grandfather loved that they named the bridge after an Italian guy.

Our house was just a few blocks away and for years we watched The Verrazano Narrows Bridge being built. We'd walk up to the end of our street and see it being formed right before our eyes. It's not every day someone builds one of the longest bridges in the world a block away from your house. My dad used to explain what was happening. I remember huge steel loops, like the eye of a sewing needle being planted in to the humongous concrete foundations. Eventually they put the cables through those loops, and then hung them over the towers, and kept pulling them tighter and tighter. Then they placed an eight-lane highway on the cables. I don't know if it's because I watched them build it, or because it was so high and massive, but going over that bridge, which opened in 1964, always gave me butterflies in my stomach.

Because it's the closest bridge to the Atlantic Ocean of all New York City bridges it is the most vulnerable to weather."[14] If a bridge was going to be closed because it was too dangerous to cross, it was usually the Verrazano Narrows Bridge. The bridge would sway in the breeze, and I would count the minutes until we crossed it and were on land again.

One night, all my fears were realized when we were crossing the Bridge from Brooklyn to Staten Island in the middle of a sudden and unexpected blizzard. I was just fourteen years old and I was gripping the back seat as my dad slowly drove across the bridge. The highway rose higher and higher until you reached the center of the bridge, and then it became a steep decline. The wind was howling and blowing snow was hitting the windshield at hurricane strength. When we had finally reached the absolute middle of the bridge and the highest and scariest place we heard the loud boom of a tire blowout on our car. The car started swerving in the snow more than it had been, and my parents cried out, "Jesus, help us." Sheer terror gripped me. My life flashed before me. My major regret was that I had been on a diet and didn't eat that brownie at the church social that evening. As if how I looked in my jeans mattered anymore.

We sat there in the middle lane with our car flashers on. My dad couldn't go for help because he'd be blown off the bridge if he did. In 1966 we didn't have a cell phone or beepers, or any way to contact anyone. We just sat there while the wind wailed and the bridge swayed. Our only hope was that someone would be kind enough to tell someone at the toll booth that there was a pitiful family of three sitting in the middle lane in the middle of the bridge at its highest point ready to be blown off the bridge and die. I could sense my parents were concerned about our precarious situation. I knew it was just a matter of moments until we would be swept off the bridge and tumble to our deaths in the icy waters of New York Harbor. Oh, the horror of it all.

About 15 minutes later, we saw the lights of an emergency tow truck pull up behind us. I breathed a sigh of relief. When the emergency tow truck driver, a big, rough-looking guy, finally knocked on the window, I understood that the only person in New York City who was more annoyed than I was to be stuck on that bridge at the moment was the tow truck driver sent to rescue us. One thing that New Yorkers never bother with is hiding annoyance. If we're annoyed at you, you know it. He was annoyed and we knew it. Because it was freezing cold, the guy jumped in our car to get some information from my parents. This terrifyingly terse and cranky man started barking out questions as if my father had planned to have a blow out in the middle of blizzard in the middle of The Verrazano Narrows Bridge. It was at this very scary moment that my Mom turned to him, smiled, and said, "You know, sir, it's not by chance you are the one who came to fix our flat tire."

I knew what that meant. Mom was going to tell this mean monster of a man about Jesus. This man, who seemed like he would have preferred we fall off the bridge rather than have to take his tow truck and help get us to safety, was about to hear that God had ordained the moment so that she could have the opportunity to share the gospel and bring his soul to safety. I remember thinking, "*Really, Mom? On top of a swaying bridge in the middle of a blizzard? Could you please just not worry about his eternal soul right now? Please, Mom? Can someone else tell him about Jesus?*"

Of course, I didn't say one word. As she spoke, in the middle of what I was sure were the final moments of my fourteenth year of life, I could see that big, cranky and annoyed-at-us man bending his head and his heart to listen to every word she spoke. Right before my eyes, I saw him becoming soft to every word she spoke. I saw tears flowing down his grease covered, creased face. And suddenly, everything around us seemed to disappear. You'd think we were sitting on a warm and sun-drenched beach in the middle of an idyllic tropical island. I saw right there in our car — in the middle lane of the New York Verrazano Narrows Bridge, at the absolute highest point, during a raging blizzard - a big, rough-looking tow truck driver begin to weep, begin to pray and confess his sin to a loving Heavenly Father. He became a new creature in Christ. All because my loving mother never permits any circumstance keep her from telling someone about the love of God. I didn't die that day, and someday neither will that tow truck driver.

Molly's Meatball Lesson #24

Don't let the storms of your life keep you from telling others about Jesus.

God Forgives. Let Him.

There aren't enough pages in all the books I could ever write to tell you about all the people who will be in Heaven because of my mother's love for the Lord. People like Monya.

When more than nine million people are living on just 468 square miles, you have a place known as New York City. To put it into perspective, combine the number of people living in Los Angeles, Chicago, Dallas and Boston[15] and you will come close to the population of New York City alone. That's over 18,000 people per square mile. The end result? Long, long lines everywhere for everything, all day, every day. Over the years, people who have career changes that bring them to live in New York City ask me for advice. I tell them that learning to accept waiting in line is the primary survival skill you will need to live in in New York City.

This reality brings me to the story of Monya. Monya was an unkempt, skin-rashed, foul-smelling drug addict and prostitute. When she walked into a bank in Staten Island one day and saw a line with 50 people waiting, she let loose with a tirade of loud and obscenity laced complaints. It had been years since Monya cared what people thought about her, and even longer since anyone cared about Monya. She just kept talking loudly to no one in particular about how ridiculous the line was. Everyone ignored her, which was nothing new for Monya.

Monya's drug addiction had cost her everything, including her only child, a daughter. Ten years earlier, when the child was only two years old, child protective services removed her from Monya's care. Because of her drug-related binges and because she lived in a city of nine million people, Monya had lost track of her daughter, her family, and any other familiar person from her past. Monya's mistakes were eating away at her — and yet she couldn't seem to stop making them. So she lashed out at everyone, including the people standing in line at that bank.

Suddenly, a silver-haired woman in line called out to Monya, "Miss? Miss? You can get in line front of me." Monya accepted the offer. This simple act of kindness hit Monya harder than any pimp ever had. It baffled and confused her. She turned to ask the woman, "Why did you let me get in front of you?" And the woman replied, "So that I could tell you that Jesus loves you."

Monya laughed, "Jesus loves ME? You've got to be kidding! How could Jesus love me? Do you know what I've done?"

"No, I don't, but Jesus does. And He died to pay for every single mistake you've ever made. God is real and He loves you."

Monya replied, "Well, if God is real, then tell Him to let me find my daughter!"

The woman continued to speak lovingly to Monya and for some reason her words were magnetic. Before Monya left the bank, she did something she hadn't done in years: she reached out to another person. There was something about this lady that she wanted in her own life. She gave the woman her phone number and address. She also asked her to pray she could find her daughter.

Monya never expected to see the silver-haired woman again. So, imagine Monya's surprise when my mother, the silver-haired woman in the line at the bank, showed up to visit at her home a few days later. As you might expect, Monya received Christ. My mother overcame Monya's objection about not having anything to wear to church by buying Monya some new clothes. Monya was in church that next Sunday morning with a beaming face and a happy heart. Her only prayer was an impossible one: that God would help her find her child in a city filled with nine million people.

After attending church for a few weeks, Monya learned about a drug recovery program at a church located in the Bronx, another borough of New York City. She applied and was accepted by the program. She tearfully hugged her my mom and her new church family goodbye and left to enter the live-in program.

One week later, at a Bible study there, Monya overheard one of the men talking to someone about his uncle. This uncle of his had a very unusual name and it was the same name of one of Monya's uncles. She overheard the conversation and asked the man if his uncle could be the same man she remembered from her childhood. He was. And through that miraculous encounter with a distant relative she'd never met before, Monya found her own mother again. And when she found her mother, Monya found the child who had been taken from her a decade earlier. She called my mother exclaiming, "God answered my prayer! He let me find my daughter today." A coincidence? A miracle? According to Monya, a direct answer to prayer. Monya told everyone, "God heard my prayer and helped me find my daughter." My mother taught Monya that nothing is impossible for God.

In the years that followed, Monya led many people to faith in Jesus. She became part of the leadership team of that ministry in the Bronx that helped people with addictions. Mom's face was beaming on the Sunday morning that ministry presented a program at our church. She saw Monya, beautiful and smiling, stand to tell the gathered crowd what happened to her life because a kind and loving woman reached out to her in a bank lobby. She said, "Until that day, I didn't know what love was, and I didn't know Jesus loved me."

A few years later, Monya's body succumbed to the damage the many years of drug abuse had created. Her heart simply gave out. Her daughter was by Monya's side as she passed away. She told my mother that Monya's last words on earth were, "I love you, Jesus." A woman who didn't believe Jesus loved her, whispered her love for Him moments before she saw His face.

Monya's life story was rewritten all because my beautiful mother wasn't afraid or ashamed to tell Monya no matter what she had done, Jesus loved her.

Molly's Meatball Lesson #25

If you ask God to send people your way who need to hear about His love, He will send them. Never waste an opportunity to say, "Jesus loves you."

God's Heart In The Passenger Seat of A Buick

The reason my mother witnesses so freely has its root in a supernatural love that is horrified at the thought that a person might spend eternity separated from God and His love. She doesn't want anyone to perish. Sounds a great deal like her Heavenly Father who *"so loved the world that he gave his one and only Son, that whoever believes in him shall not perish but have eternal life. For God did not send his Son into the world to condemn the world, but to save the world through him"* (John 3:16-17).

It is otherworldly, desperate love that compels my mother. She cannot keep herself from explaining the wonder of walking through life with the love and presence of God. God is as real to her as the person she is talking to. No, that's not accurate. God is more real than any person she knows. She loves people and she wants them to understand that God loves them. She isn't trying to get brownie points with God. She just loves people. It's just pure, simple and holy love.

My mom and I went out recently. One of our stops was at her doctor's office for her annual routine check-up. Her doctor adores her. Everyone does. At her first visit with him she told him, "Doctor, I'm going to pray for you. What should I pray about?" And whether or not he has a prayer request, she takes his hand, and prays out loud for him. She prays that God will give him wisdom and compassion for his patients. She asks for him to have clear thoughts and for supernatural strength. When she is finished praying, then he can begin doctoring. That's just the way it is. Once, we were leaving and my mom hadn't started to pray yet, and the doctor said, "Miss Molly, where's my prayer?"

As with so many people, I watch as the power of God inside this feisty little 92 year old brings reverence and respect for the God she is praying to. He bows his head. She prays as long as she wants to pray. While other people complain about having to wait for their doctors, my mother's doctor respectfully waits for her to finish praying for him.

After her prayer on this recent visit, he said to her, "Miss Molly, we're going to take some blood as part of your check up today." He took her by the hand, and slowly walked her to the lab department. This task is usually reserved for an aid or office worker. I could see the surprise on the faces of the people who work in his practice that the doctor himself was personally walking her down the long hallway to get her blood drawn. My mother was waving at everyone as if she was in the Macy's Thanksgiving Day Parade. We arrived at our destination in the lab and the doctor handed her off to the lab tech by saying, "Take care of our Miss Molly" and walked away after she made him bend down so she could hug him.

The lab technician was a pretty woman, about 40 years old with streaked and spiked blonde hair, who said, "Good afternoon, Miss Molly. How are you doing today?" My mother saw a butterfly tattoo on the woman's wrist as she was searching for a vein in my mother's arm. My mom pointed to it and said, "Oh, that's pretty. Didn't that hurt when they were doing that?" She is still *very* curious about *everything.* The lab test faded in to the background as Molly and the woman became friends. The woman stopped and talked about her tattoo.

And then, as I knew she would, my mother got around to the gospel. She started with her usual questions, "What church do you go to?" and the woman said, "I don't go to church. I don't like the people who go to church. I stopped going years ago." My mother agreed that church people can hurt you sometimes, but she assured the woman that Jesus will never hurt us.

The woman responded, "I don't really want any religion. I'm good without it."

"Oh, but Jesus loves you so much", my mother said with compassion in her voice.

"OK, that's fine."

"Do you understand what He did for you?"

"I appreciate your concern," she said firmly, "but I do not want Jesus in my life. I do not want Jesus."

My mother's face turned white as a ghost. She couldn't believe what she was hearing. I don't think she's ever heard those words before. Her face spoke volumes to me. How could this be? Someone was rejecting Jesus? How could this be true? But it was true. For the rest of their moments together, my mother was polite and loving to her.

We checked out at the front desk. A few minutes later we were back in the car and on our way to our next appointment for the day. I had forgotten about the lab technician's woman words. As I drove, I happened to glance at my mother. She was sitting there in silence while huge tears were rolling down her face.

"Mom, what's wrong?"

"What will she do without Jesus? How will she live without Jesus? She will be separated from God forever. She cannot see God unless she goes through Jesus. Does she understand this? She is rejecting the love she is longing for." And the tears, as big as her broken heart, rolled down her face.

In that holy moment, I knew I was seeing the very heart of God sitting next to me in the passenger seat of a Buick. I was seeing God's heart for humanity: Pleading, calling, wanting none to perish. Offering deep and holy love. Not angry and vengeful but brokenhearted and mournful when anyone rejects His Only Son. It's been three weeks and she is still praying for the woman to come to Christ. She is asking everyone she knows to pray for her. Will you pray for her? We don't know her name, but God does.

"There is more joy in heaven over one lost sinner who repents and returns to God than over ninety-nine others who are righteous and haven't strayed away!"

— LUKE 15:7, NLT

Molly's Meatball Lesson #26

If you don't pray for the people you know who don't know Jesus — who will?

4

MIRROR, MIRROR

The Recipe For Reading and Understanding The Bible

*"For the word of God is quick and powerful and sharper than
any two edged sword, piercing even to the dividing asunder of soul
and spirit, and of the joints and marrow and is a discerner of the
thoughts and intents of the heart."*

— HEBREWS 4:12, KJV

I've struggled with writing this chapter because I could write a book
about The Book and how it has shaped and influenced everything about
my existence on this planet. No matter how many words I write, I could
write more about how God's Word has sustained my parents and sharp-
ened their faith. My parents, married for 72 years, recite Hebrews 4:12
in unison every night before they fall asleep. My son has recorded them
doing this on his smart phone because it's the most wonderful thing in
the world to see two people in their nineties reciting Bible verses to one
another. In my parents I have seen lives that do more than committing
God's word to memory. It's like they are memorizing their marching or-
ders from their heavenly Commander in Chief. If the Bible says it, they

believe it and they live what they believe. It's a simple and powerful way to live life. My parents are proof that the Bible is more than just a book. No one can read the same Book for seven or eight decades and STILL FIND it life giving and life changing. And while it's important to do what the Word says, she continues to take the time to hide it in her heart. At the moment, she is almost finished memorizing John Chapter 17. The entire chapter.

Molly's Meatball Lesson #27

There is no age limit on memorizing Scripture. Do it with your children and your grandchildren. And keep doing it until you see the Lord.

Mirror, Mirror On The Table

Do not merely listen to the word, and so deceive yourselves. Do what it says. Anyone who listens to the word but does not do what it says is like someone who looks at his face in a mirror and after looking at himself, goes away and immediately forgets what he looks like. But whoever looks intently into the perfect law that gives freedom, and continues in it—not forgetting what they have heard, but doing it—they will be blessed in what they do."

— JAMES 1:22-25

If there's a flat surface in my parent's home, there is most certainly a Bible on it. My mother's Bible is the cornerstone of her life. It is well-read and worn. (It's in the last scene of the movie *War Room* by the Kendrick Brothers. Yes, my mother's well-read and well-worn Bible made it in to the movie. More on that later.) Every day, before she does anything else, Mom reads the Bible. Every morning, with her morning coffee, she sits and talks to God. And then she opens her Bible to hear what God has to say to her. She will turn to the Psalm that corresponds with the day of the month. (If it's the 4th of the month, she reads Psalm 4.) And then she reads what she feels like reading. Her faith is such that she believes God is big enough to speak specifically to her through His Word. Every morning she waits for a specific Scripture to jump out at her. And when it does, she writes that verse down on a white index card. Without fail, sometime during the day that very verse is the one she uses to encourage someone she speaks to on the phone or sees in person. As I've already written, her primary prayer each day is "Lord, send someone in to my life today that I can tell about You." And every day, without fail, that verse she has written down is EXACTLY the verse someone she speaks to is needing to hear. She is armed and ready with her Sword.

I saw my mom treat the Bible as a spiritual mirror. Whatever our personal opinion of ourselves, God's Word always tells us truth about who and what we really are in His sight. If a person believes she is without sin and does not need God's forgiveness, the Bible tells her just the opposite: *"All have sinned and come short of the glory of God"* (Rom. 3:23, KJV). If someone feels unworthy of God's love and forgiveness, or believes she has gone too far or done too much wrong, the Bible tells us that God is longing to show mercy and forgive her sin. *"Come now, let us settle the matter,"* says the Lord, *"Though your sins are like scarlet, they shall be as white as snow, though they are red as crimson, they shall be like wool"* (Isa. 1:18).

Some people are afraid to see themselves by the standard God sets in His Word. And it is a high and different standard than we see in the world every day. Some people, usually those who have never really read the Bible, believe it says that first you clean up your act and then you can bother God with your mess. But the Bible says just the opposite. Bring your mess to God and He will clean up your act for you. The Bible reveals God's heart for you and His love for you and His plans for you. But first you have to read it.

Molly's Meatball Lesson #28

Read the Bible. Then do what it says.

Not Letting Go

"They came to him, clasped his feet and worshiped him."

— MATTHEW 28:9

I call her every morning. And possibly another 10 or 20 times during the day. That's just our routine, to start the day checking on one another and share whatever happens to one of us all through the day. On a recent morning, as I was getting ready to work on writing this chapter, I called her on the phone. Her voice sounded like she'd been crying. She was emotional, for sure. I asked, "What's wrong, Mom?"

"Nothing's wrong. I was reading Matthew, Chapter 28. Jesus had died and had been buried. Can you imagine the hopelessness the disciples were feeling? They thought He was dead. They felt despondent and alone. Wait, let me read it to you." Mom dropped the phone and I heard her rustling the pages of her Bible. I heard her rustling the pages of her Bible to read the angel's words to me, *"He is not here; he has risen, just as he said. Come and see the place where he lay'* (v. 6). Marie, can you imagine how they felt? They must have been so confused thinking "What? He's not dead? Where is He?" And then as they walked, He appeared to them. And the Bible says they fell to the ground and grabbed and clasped His feet. *"So the women hurried away from the tomb, afraid yet filled with joy, and ran to tell his disciples. Suddenly Jesus met them. "Greetings," he said. They came to him, clasped his feet and worshiped him"'* (vv. 8-9). Marie, they must have been thinking, 'We won't let You go again. We want to hold on to You forever.' They didn't want to let Him go. They didn't want to let Him go. And I was telling Jesus this morning that I am clinging to Him just as tightly. I don't want to let Him go. I just want to be at His feet. I just love Him. I just love Him."

"Yes, Mom, I know you do."

And that's how reading the Bible works in the life of my mother. It isn't some book she reads because she's supposed to read it. To her, the Bible is God speaking to her. It's a real and living Word from God every morning.

And on that morning, it inspired her to fall in love with Jesus. Again. And hearing her absolute affection for Him, remembering the truth that we Christians believe that He actually rose from death, hearing the hope in her voice that Jesus is real and Someone she wants to cling to, inspires me to feel the same thing she is feeling.

Molly's Meatball Lesson #29

Read the Bible like it's a love letter from God Himself.
Because that's exactly what it is.

Being Good Is Not Enough

"It is by grace you have been saved, through faith – and this is not from yourselves, it is the gift of God not by works, so that no one can boast."

— EPHESIANS 2:8-9

Someday, when eternity begins, I would like to meet the person who handed my grandfather, Pellegrino Signorelli, a Salvation Army tract. The year was about 1917, in the Mulberry Street section of Manhattan. I imagine this person had handed out hundreds of tracts to the Italian immigrants who had gathered together in the new land they had chosen. And this simple act of spreading the gospel changed the eternal future of our family. I never met my grandfather, but from what I've heard from my mom, he lived a bold and fearless life of proclaiming the gospel. God reached down to this powerful man and changed his mind about what God cares about, how God deals with people, and how much God loves sinners. And it was the Bible's power that did that. A verse on that tract so intrigued my grandfather that he decided to visit the church whose name was stamped on the back. He saw the truth in God's Word. After a lifetime of religion, the Holy Spirit made the Bible come alive and my grandfather understood that salvation and being right with God *"does not, therefore, depend on human desire or effort, but on God's mercy"* (Rom. 9:16).

My grandparents were raised in a religion that required a person to constantly keep track of every sin that had been committed. This sin was washed away once a week when that person confessed the sin, made atonement for that sin through prayers and other things, and attended church and took communion. As Italians, it was difficult to know where the Italian culture stopped and the religion started. It was just part of who they were.

As my grandfather heard and read the Bible for the very first time, he finally understood that no one is able to earn salvation from God. No one can be good enough. No one. Not you. Not me. Not my grandfather. Not my mother. Religion is a bunch of rules that a bunch of people have created in order to assuage their guilty conscience.

In the Garden of Eden, when sin first entered the human race, the first thing Adam and Eve did was to hide from God. And if we'd be honest with ourselves, most of us are still hiding from Him. We all know deep inside that we have fallen short of a holy and righteous God. And so we avoid Him. As if He doesn't see us. We convince ourselves that if we stop doing things we know are wrong, and if we start doing things we know are right, that somehow this will impress God and He will make us His child. But this isn't the truth.

My grandfather fully embraced God's grace, but my grandmother did not. She had a room devoted to various saints and the statues representing them. She believed they were the mediators between God and people. However she could not deny that something had changed in my grandfather. He became someone who *did* what the Bible said he should do. Over the next several months, she saw a change that seemed to be coming from the inside out. One day, after my grandfather left for work, she said to herself, "I am going to look at that book he is always reading." She opened his Bible and it fell open at John 14:6: "Jesus answered, 'I am the way and the truth and the life. No one comes to the Father except through me." This Scripture hit her straight in the heart of the matter. My grandmother often told us that her first thoughts after reading this verse was, "If Jesus is the ONLY way to the Father, then what am I doing with all these saints in the other room?" She started attending church with my grandfather because rather than quoting the Bible in front of her, he lived it. My mother says her mother always told her that she knew the Bible was powerful because after my grandfather started reading it and everything about him changed – because he started doing what the Bible told him to do.

Molly's Meatball Lesson #30

Live the Bible more than you quote it.

Being Good Is Not Enough Because We Cannot Be Good Enough

> *"In fact, the law requires that nearly everything be cleansed with blood, and without the shedding of blood there is no forgiveness."*

— HEBREWS 9:22

The Bible was the Book that changed my grandfather, my grandmother and eventually, my mother. In spite of her parents' devotion to living the Word more than just reading it, when my mom was a young adult, she had a holy "mirror moment" of her own. She admits that as a pastor's daughter, surrounded by church people, living in a Christian family, she kind of felt like she had always just loved God, because, well, she always had. She felt like she had always been "saved." And one day, while reading the Bible, God got her attention in a very unusual way. She was reading Hebrews, Chapter 9.

This book was written to Jewish Christians. They are the foundation of Christianity. And they were being persecuted for their faith. As my grandparents discovered, it isn't easy to deal with people who are steeped in religious customs. Religious people like the status quo. The writer of Hebrews hints that maybe some of these early Christians might be growing weary of the persecution and martyrdom of their faith and were thinking of going back to their old religious ways.

My mother was a little bit of a religious girl without realizing it. But that day, as she read these words, *"How much more then will the blood of Christ who through the eternal Spirit offered himself unblemished to God, cleanse our consciences from acts that lead to death, so that we may serve the living God!"* (Heb. 9:14), something supernatural stirred in her innermost being. It began to dawn on her in a profound way that God was not impressed with Molly, or her family, or her church, or her holy living. God was not changing His mind about sin. God required a sacrifice – even for Molly – and that was that. And then something unusual happened. As if to be sure she got the memo, she recalls, "As I read the Bible, it's like the words came off the page and were floating in the air. I saw the words, 'without shedding of blood is no remission' floating in the air before my eyes. As if God wanted to be sure that I understood that the only thing that would make me clean and holy and acceptable in the sight of God was and is the blood of Jesus. I understood in a moment that God was requiring Someone to pay for my sin. And I understood that being from a godly family was not enough. Being good is not enough because we cannot be good enough. It was and is the blood of Jesus that paid for Molly's sin. I made things right with God that day. After all those years of growing up in church it hit me that Jesus died for me because I needed a sacrifice to pay for my sin. And Jesus is that sacrifice."

Molly's Meatball Lesson #31

Jesus died for your sin whether you believe that or not.

Mom's Bible is worn, well-used and the words inside it have shaped her life and mine. I could write volumes more… but… I am moving on to the funny side of Molly Bruno.

5

HAND BEAT 300 TIMES

The Recipe For Laughter

"The fruit of the Spirit is…. JOY!"

— GALATIANS 5:22

The funny thing about my mother is how funny she is. She is genuinely, authentically and hilariously hilarious. You cannot be around her for long without finding yourself in a happy, laughing moment or two. She reminds me a little of Lucille Ball. To witness her absolute holy power, amazing answers to prayer, utter devotion to God *and* the most sidesplitting and unbelievable mishaps packaged into the same 5'2" woman is what makes Molly Bruno truly one-of-a-kind. My greatest memory of her will be the laughter and the joy. The laughter. The joy. I will always remember the moments we caught each other's eye somewhere, read each other's thoughts, and could not stop laughing until one of us got up and left the room. I cannot count the times one or the other of us confessed after an event, "I couldn't look at you or I would have laughed so much I would have embarrassed myself."

I suspect the reason I am sometimes invited to various gatherings is to be the entertainment. Invariably, before the night comes to an end, someone will say, "Tell us some stories about your mother." And that's it for the rest of the night. People are laughing until they cry. The anecdotes you are about to read are all true. I have witnesses. I do. You should know that the person who laughs the loudest at them is my mom. Even *she* thinks she's funny. I shared "The Sniper Story" in chapter one. Would you like to read about "The Cake Story?"

The Cake Story

My mom is an excellent cook, especially when it comes to Italian food. And contrary to what you may (or may not) believe about Americans with Italian ancestry, we do not eat pasta at every meal. We want to. We just don't. Every now and then when the boat from Naples is delayed, we might eat chicken, mashed potatoes, vegetables, or even a fruit. But mind you, only if we are forced to.

Just like many families, when I was growing up, our family activity was centered in and around our kitchen. In the afternoons after school, I often sat there watching mom prepare dinner while I did my homework. Sometimes she would give me an assignment such as slicing the carrots or setting the table. Dinner was a great big deal in our home. My brother Nick and I knew that every night at 5:30, dinner would be piping hot and on our kitchen table ready for us to devour. We wouldn't think about being one minute late. We weren't *allowed* to be one minute late.

After we had finished eating, all four of us lingered at the table catching up with one another's day. There have been books written and television documentaries about the positive effect of a family having dinner together every night. I agree. For me, that evening dinner table was the one sure thing in my day every day. Because I love to talk, I knew I would have my parents' undivided attention. My father would ask each of us, "How was your day?" and of course, that's all he had to say. I was off and running.

I must say that Mom's kitchen spoke love to me. I saw the love she put into preparing the meals for us. But I do suffer from what I have named "Dessert Deprivation Disorder." My mom didn't bake. Couldn't bake. Wouldn't bake. Some of my friends have special times with their grandchildren baking cookies, cakes and pies from recipes their mother taught them. Passing the precious sweetness on to the next generation. Not me. If we wanted a cake or a pie or cookie, we bought it. We survived.

But Mom's sister, my Aunt Brady, was an excellent baker, always making some kind of cake for her family. When I was a newlywed, my mom and I visited her one day in her beautiful, antique filled home. She served us a delicious, warm pound cake. We wanted more. Aunt Brady said, "Molly, you can make this cake. It's the simplest thing in the world. She copied the recipe and gave it to my mom, encouraging her again, "Molly, you can do this."

The very next day, with great anticipation and excitement in her voice, Mom announced to me on the phone, "I'm baking that pound cake today. I bought all the ingredients at the store yesterday." I was shocked. My mom? Baking? She said, "Come on over and have some cake. It should be ready by the time you get here."

I drove over and walked into a scene straight out of an "I Love Lucy" episode. My mother had cake batter all over her clothing, hair, hands, and arms up to her elbows pus all over the kitchen table and floor.

"MOM! What happened??"

"I'm never baking again. All this mess and trouble just to eat a piece of cake? No wonder I never bake."

"Mom, how did you get cake batter all over you?"

"How could I NOT get it all over me? The recipe says, 'Hand beat 300 times.' So I beat the batter with my hands 300 times!" She demonstrated a karate chop beating style she had used inside the bowl filled with cake batter.

"Let me get this straight." I said, trying to keep a straight face, "You kept whacking the batter with your hands 300 times? You counted until you reached 300 whacks?"

"Yes."

She had a perplexed look on her face as she saw me losing my breath from laughter. She wasn't too happy about me laughing at her. Finally, when I could catch my breath long enough to speak, I explained, "Mom, it doesn't mean to literally beat the batter with your hands. It means mix the batter thoroughly with a spoon and not an electric mixer."

"Then why does it say, 'hand beat 300 times' if it actually means 'don't use an electric mixer but a spoon?' I did what it said to do."

She hardly had any cake batter left to bake. What came out of the oven was more the size of a large cookie than a pound cake. It was not tasty at all. She never tried to bake anything again for the rest of her life. For this we, her family, are thankful.

Molly's Meatball Lesson #32

Don't expect to be an expert at everything. Know your own limitations.
There's nothing wrong with acknowledging that some tasks are better left to others.

And If You Ever Almost Blow Up The House....

Speaking of cooking and kitchens, my mom had two full kitchens in our home on Staten Island. It had been my grandparents' house. When my dad grew up and moved away, they converted their one family house into a two family unit. This is not unusual in New York City. Most homes have at least two separate living quarters. My grandparents rented out the top floor for extra income, and they lived on the lower level. As they aged and became too weak to care for themselves, my parents and I (my brother was away at college) moved into the upstairs part of the house. When both my grandparents left us to live in Heaven, we converted the two levels back into one big house. The lower level became like a finished basement with a full kitchen and the upper level was where we actually lived.

My mom liked to cook in the downstairs kitchen so that the upstairs kitchen would stay clean. She is a meticulous housekeeper. On one particular day she was home alone. She went downstairs to preheat the oven. The preheating process on that older gas stove involved turning a knob that turned on the gas. Then you had to physically light a match, put it in a small hole in the bottom of the oven, near where the gas vapors were pouring out, and be sure that the fire ignited. My mom turned the knob, but didn't notice that the match she used did not ignite the fire. She went upstairs and continued working. About 30 minutes later, Mom went down to put the roast in the oven and smelled the heavy smell of gas. She realized that the oven had never lighted. So what did she do? Turn the oven off and open all the windows? No, my mom stood in a room filled with the heavy smell of gas and struck a match to light the oven. She recalls, "I heard a loud noise, and the next thing I knew I was up against the wall on the other side of the room (a distance of about 20 feet). I was as high as the ceiling and I was sliding down the wall. I was on fire. I ran out of the house into the middle of the street." A few of her neighbors happened to be outside and helped her put out the flames.

When I got home later that day, I immediately noticed that she had no eyebrows at all. There were some slight burn marks on her forehead and nose and her hairline was at least an inch further back than it was when I left the house that morning to go to school. The thing that consumed Mom's thoughts was, "One minute I was lighting the oven, the next minute I was on fire and sliding down the wall on the other side of the room. In the twinkling of an eye, I could have been standing before the Lord. And so could all of my neighbors." In the weeks that followed, as her eyebrows and hair line grew back she made her way to every one of her neighbors to make sure they knew that in the twinkling of an eye they could be face to face with their Creator – especially on those nights she might be cooking a roast.

Molly's Meatball Lesson # 33

Don't assume you will see tomorrow.
Live each day as if it is your last because it might be.

Atomic Power

"The one who is in you is greater than the one who is in the world."

— 1 JOHN 4:4

"For the kingdom of God is not a matter of talk but of power."

— 1 CORINTHIANS 4:20

My husband, our son, and I lived near Harrisburg, Pennsylvania, for a number of years. It's a small city in the central part of the state located on the Susquehanna River and near the beautiful farmlands of Pennsylvania. We loved living there. In March of 1979, while our family was in Los Angeles for an extended visit we were astounded to see Harrisburg on the evening news. The nuclear power plant located on Three Mile Island was in danger of having a complete meltdown. As a result of this near catastrophic event, Three Mile Island was the focus of almost constant news media attention for weeks following. Thankfully, they contained the problem before it became uncontainable and widely destructive. My mom watched the news from her home in New York. Especially interested because it was happening in the city we lived in. After a few weeks the story died down and left the headlines.

A year or two later, while she and my dad were visiting us in Pennsylvania, they met some friends of ours who had recently relocated to Harrisburg. The guy was a nuclear scientist who had been hired to train the operators at Three Mile Island. This was a very high level job. I'm sure his technical title is not "this guy was a nuclear scientist" but you get the idea. My mom, who is naturally curious about every single thing on earth, was very curious about Three Mile Island. Over dinner, he answered all her questions about what happened in1979 and explained the basics of nuclear power. She asked a classic "Molly question" that evening, saying, "Now that you mention it, I have always wondered, where is this atom and why does everyone keep splitting it?"

Being the nice guy that he was he tried to explain about protons and neutrons, but she didn't grasp what he was saying. Finally he offered her a rare opportunity. He asked, "Would you like to tour the facility? Would you like to see the controls?" Her eyes lit up. She's always ready for a new adventure. She immediately accepted his offer.

A few days later, we drove on to Three Mile Island, a small island in the Susquehanna River. When we drove past those huge and famous concrete towers, Mom's eyes were open wide as those of a child driving into Disney World for the first time. It takes a lot to impress someone who lives in the same city as the Statue of Liberty and the Empire State Building, but she was impressed. Security on the island was tight and we made it through the gate. We parked our cars and walked into the building. When we got to the entry door, Mom took the arm of our friend in an effort to stop him from going any farther. Then she said to him, "Before we go inside I want to ask you something. Is the power of God within me going to affect all this nuclear power here? I don't want to cause any problems. I don't want another meltdown." This scientist friend didn't understand what Mom had asked him. He said, "Excuse me?" She repeated, "The power of God that lives inside me is very, very powerful. Is it going to affect the nuclear power on this island? I don't want to cause any problems." He glanced at me with a "Is she kidding?" look on his face. I shrugged. What do you say about a woman who so completely honors the power of God inside her that she thinks she's going to set off warning signals and possibly cause another meltdown at a nuclear power plant?

He replied, "No. No. We'll be fine."

And with that she continued walking in the door, confident that the measly nuclear power running the power plant and providing power for millions of homes and businesses would be safe from Greater Power living inside her.

Molly's Meatball Lesson #34

Always remember if you are a child of God, God's power walks into every room you walk into. Every other power must bow to the power of God within you.

Amalie? Molly? Emily? Condo?

My grandparents wanted their children to be diligent in their studies, but as Italian immigrants, their knowledge of American school systems and English was limited. My grandfather insisted that his children learn English fluently and become Americans in every way. While we were always taught that being Italian was the most wonderful thing a person could ever be (and I am proud to be a woman with Italian ancestry), my grandfather's attitude was that if he wanted his children to cling to their Italian ways and customs, he would have stayed in Italy. He was adamant that they attend school and become Americans.

When my grandfather registered my mother for kindergarten he did not have enough command of English to understand that when he spoke her actual name, "Amalie" they thought he said "Emily." All through her school years, Mom's classmates called her Emily. She just rolled with it. Maybe that's why she doesn't feel bad about not quite getting *your* name right. If your name is Tim she might call you Tom, or if it's Anna and she calls you Ann, that's close enough for her. As a woman who went through her school years responding to a name that wasn't hers, she isn't going to let you make a big deal out of just one letter and doesn't understand why anyone would.

One incorrect letter here or there didn't matter much to Mom until a week after the New York City Marathon. The week earlier, as happens every November, the New York City Marathon plots its course through all five boroughs. In order to include Staten Island, the organizers start the race at the Verrazano Narrows Bridge. My parents' house was a half block away from the tollbooths. So every year, on the Sunday morning of the Marathon, there were thousands upon thousands of runners and news media surrounding the neighborhood. Because of the traffic and the media surrounding the event, it was often impossible for my parents to get to church.

Never one to miss an opportunity to tell someone about Jesus, Mom would stand outside her front door and offer the runners her home to use if they wanted something to drink or to use the restroom. Hundreds of runners accepted her generous offer. As they did, she told them about

God's generous offer to forgive them and welcome them into His family. Some people took her name and number and actually called her back weeks later to discuss the Gospel.

One year, on the Sunday after the Marathon, my husband and I were invited to travel from Harrisburg and share music and speak at the Sunday morning services for the church in Staten Island where my father was the assistant pastor. After the service, there were quite a few members standing in the lobby with Mom and with me. One of the women half-jokingly mentioned that I shouldn't ever, ever think of having "Sister Molly" move to Pennsylvania and away from them.

Upon hearing this, my mom said, "No. I don't want to leave Staten Island. I don't want to move. But you know, last week a marathon runner who used our home left me his card in case we might consider selling our house. He just got a new job in Manhattan and he and his family are looking for a place to live. He loved our home. He can't afford to live in Manhattan. I didn't realize this, but he told me that in Manhattan, a tiny condom sells for almost $750,000."

Everyone in the lobby gasped. "Sister Molly!!"

"What? What? What's wrong?"

"Mom, I think you meant to say *condo*."

I whispered in her ear the difference between what she meant to say and what she said.

Her face got red and she said, "Oh, well. You knew what I meant."

And actually we did.

(FYI: I asked my mom, "Do you think anyone might be offended if I include this story about you? Do you mind if I put it in or should I leave it out?" Her response, "It's the truth. It happened. Put it in.")

Molly's Meatball Lesson #35

If you did it, admit it.

Would You Like a Screwdriver?

A new hair salon opened in our neighborhood. They had a Grand Opening and encouraged walk-ins to come in for a free wash, dry, and style. Everything was free. They offered food and drinks. My mother decided to check it out. The place was crowded with customers. My mom was welcomed with great appreciation. She was told she'd have to wait about ten minutes to get her hair done. While she waited, someone asked her if she'd like a beer, wine, a martini, or a screwdriver. She said she'd like a screwdriver. She knew my dad loved new tools.

While she waited for the screwdriver, someone handed her a drink. "Oh, no, thank you." The person took the drink back.

Someone else passed by and saw her sitting there and offered some beer, wine, a martini, or a screwdriver. Once again she agreed to receive a screwdriver. Once again, someone brought her a drink. This happened three times before she understood that a screwdriver is the name of a drink and *not* a tool for screwing and unscrewing screws.

In order to write about all her funny mishaps, I'm thinking I might have to write a sequel titled, "How To Make A FUNNY Meatball." If these stories made you smile, that would make her smile. Seeing my mother's smile is seeing the most wonderful thing her daughter can ever see.

Molly's Meatball Lesson #36

*The best way to deal with people laughing at your mistakes
is to laugh along with them.*

6

GIVE ME A KISS AND SLEEP IN PEACE

The Recipe For Being A Daughter

"Honor your father and your mother, so that you may live long in
the land
the LORD *your God is giving you."*

— EXODUS 20:12

One of the primary relationship lessons my mother taught me started with the most basic one: how to be a daughter. Actually, a better way of phrasing that is: how to honor my parents. This lesson was foundational before I could learn how to be a wife, mother, a follower of Jesus or a grandmother. I learned how to honor my parents by observing the way my mother honored hers. Honoring your parents? Do people actually still care about that? They should.

Even if you haven't read the Bible, you've most certainly seen the movie, *The Ten Commandments.* The people are in slavery and God uses Charlton Heston...uhh...Moses to deliver them from it. Pretty quickly after the exodus and the whole splitting the Red Sea miracle, God stops them long enough so that Moses can climb the mountaintop and have a sit down meeting with God, who decides to reveal Himself to Moses and a bunch of former slaves schlepping through the desert. What an honor for them. He calls these people "My people." He went through all the trouble of sending a deliverer, and so now He wants to set some ground rules about how to thrive and survive in a healthy kind of community. In order to help them accomplish this, He gives Moses "The Top Ten List Of Rules For Co-Existing With Other Human Beings" also known as The Ten Commandments. God chose to confine this important list of commandments to only ten. And smack dab in the middle of these Ten Commandments is #5:"Honor your father and your mother." Really? Really. He listed that commandment *before* "do not kill," "do not steal," and "do not commit adultery."

Honor. It means to realize the value of something and to acknowledge it. It means the opposite of dishonor. When Jesus was speaking to some holier-than-thou religious leaders of His day who were accusing Him of not following tradition by the way He and His disciples washed their hands, He pointed out that while they were getting all upset about a man-made tradition, they were breaking one of the Ten Commandments by not honoring their parents. Even 2,000 years ago, for some reason, people had already begun ignoring this commandment of God. Jesus reminded them, *"For God said, 'Honor your father and mother' and 'Anyone who curses their father or mother is to be put to death"* (Matt. 13:4).

Evidently, there is something so intrinsically destructive to a society that allows its children to dishonor their own parents that God made it carry the ultimate sentence – death. Curse your parents and you die. Really? Really. God was making it clear that when a blind eye is turned to children who do not honor and obey their parents, such behavior will corrupt that society as much as stealing, killing, committing adultery and bearing false witness against someone when that society turns a blind eye to children who do not honor, obey and respect their parents. Really? Really.

The apostle Paul foresaw a period in history he referred to as "the last days." Sadly, these words don't sound like something that will happen in our future but seems to describe what is happening now: *"But mark this: There will be terrible times in the last days. People will be lovers of themselves, lovers of money, boastful, proud, abusive, disobedient to their parents, ungrateful, unholy, without love, unforgiving, slanderous, without self-control, brutal, not lovers of the good, treacherous, rash, conceited, lovers of pleasure rather than lovers of God— having a form of godliness but denying its power. Have nothing to do with such people"* (2 Tim. 3:1-5). In his list of what constituted "terrible times," Paul included people who are "disobedient to their parents." Maybe we think that adulterers, thieves or murderers ruin society more than those who fail to honor, respect and obey his or her parents. However, God didn't make that distinction. He wrote these commandments with His own finger in two tablets of stone. And God's finger wrote the words, *"Honor your father and mother."*

In the world in which I grew up, children were seen but not heard. That meant they didn't interrupt adults when they were speaking. I don't think I've got any deep emotional scars because I was taught to respect what was going on when adults were involved. And speaking of speaking, I never once heard my mom say, "Because I said so!" Why? Because I would not have had the nerve to question one thing she instructed. I knew better than to talk back to Mom while Dad was around. I never even tried to get sassy or disrespectful with my father because Molly would have his back in one moment and my bottom the next. She insisted that I learn how to honor her and my father as my parents. Why? Because God commanded it. And who is supposed to teach a child to respect his or her parents? The child's parents.

Molly's Meatball Lesson #37

Teaching a child that parents deserve honor is not an option.
It's a commandment.

"Yes, Mom."

I can completely relate to the following story of Jesus and His Jewish mother because the only thing comparable to a Jewish mother is an Italian mother. Here's the way the Bible tells the story: *"On the third day a wedding took place at Cana in Galilee. Jesus' mother was there, and Jesus and his disciples had also been invited to the wedding. When the wine was gone, Jesus' mother said to him, 'They have no more wine.' 'Woman, why do you involve me?' Jesus replied. 'My hour has not yet come.' His mother said to the servants, 'Do whatever he tells you.' Nearby stood six stone water jars, the kind used by the Jews for ceremonial washing, each holding from twenty to thirty gallons. Jesus said to the servants, 'Fill the jars with water'; so they filled them to the brim. Then he told them, 'Now draw some out and take it to the master of the banquet.' They did so, and the master of the banquet tasted the water that had been turned into wine. He did not realize where it had come from, though the servants who had drawn the water knew. Then he called the bridegroom aside and said, 'Everyone brings out the choice wine first and then the cheaper wine after the guests have had too much to drink; but you have saved the best till now.' What Jesus did here in Cana of Galilee was the first of the signs through which he revealed his glory; and his disciples believed in him"* (John 2:1-11).

This story reminds me of the life I lived with my mother. Well, not exactly. I have never turned water in to wine (though my mother would tell me that through Christ I am able to). And I'm not comparing Molly Bruno to Mary, the mother of Jesus, but I can relate to this story.

First of all, His mother knew what Jesus could do and wasn't afraid to encourage Him to use the gifts of the Holy Spirit dwelling inside Him. Secondly, she was clearly overstepping her boundaries by involving Him in the situation because He pointedly told her, "My hour has not yet come" (v. 4). She ignored His protests. *"His mother said to the servants, 'Do whatever he tells you'"* (v. 5).

At this point the story could have gone another way. He could have held His ground. After all, He was God in human flesh. If anyone had the right to pull rank on His mother, it was Jesus. If anyone could have said, "Don't tell Me what to do, Mom," it was Jesus, The very Son of God. Instead it was a "Yes, Mom" moment for Jesus. Jesus showed great respect for His mother. He honored her and did what she asked Him to do. Not only that, He did it well. He made His mother proud. The wine He made from water was better than the wine that was being served at first. My opinion is that Jesus did that for His mom just because she was His mom.

And this miracle was the first He ever publicly performed, causing His disciples to believe in Him. Isn't it amazing how a 'Yes, Mom' attitude can change the world around you.

My "Yes, Mom" moments have not been moments when I performed mighty miracles like turning water in to wine and my mother certainly didn't give birth to a perfect child like Mary did. But because I was taught to honor her, I have reluctantly acquiesced to things I didn't really feel like doing. Things like singing a song to someone named Susan, a total stranger, in a restaurant. I mean, as you might be able to guess, I'm not shy about speaking or singing in public. But, really, this time, in this restaurant, I would have preferred silence. I don't remember how Mom began talking to Susan about the Lord. Susan was sitting at the next table. As most people do right after meeting Molly, Susan opened up to my mother. It turns out she was overcome with crippling guilt. I tried to act like I didn't hear her say to Susan, "You should hear my daughter's song, 'He Has Forgiven Me.'[16] Marie, sing the song for Susan. My daughter has the most beautiful voice. Marie, sing your song!" She turned and looked at me and I tried to get away with not looking at her, at making believe I didn't hear her. She's my mom. I didn't fool her. "Marie?"

I thought, "What Mom? Here? In this restaurant? Now?" I didn't *want* to sing the song for Susan. I didn't *have* to sing the song for Susan. I was in my 40s. I didn't have to obey. I gave her a look that said, "Really, Mom?" She gave me a look that said, "Really." I sang the song for Susan. My mother used to say, "In the amount of time it took you to explain to me why you can't or won't do it, you could have done it." Yes, Mom. In the amount of time Jesus would have used to explain why He didn't want to turn the water in to wine, He did it.

Three years later, in the middle of dying for the sins of humanity, being beaten beyond human appearance, enduring when His Father turned His face from Him, Jesus was not too preoccupied that it caused Him to forget about His mother being honored and cared for. Scripture says, *"Near the cross of Jesus stood his mother, his mother's sister, Mary the wife of Clopas, and Mary Magdalene. When Jesus saw his mother there, and the disciple whom he loved standing nearby, he said to her, 'Woman here is your son,' and to the disciple,*

'Here is your mother.' From that time on, this disciple took her into his home" (John 19:25-27).

As my parents have aged and needed more care, I have adjusted my life to their needs rather than adjusting their needs to my life. It isn't convenient. It isn't fun to actually lay down your actual life for another person – even the person who gave your life. It's just what I witnessed as I was growing up. It's part of honoring my godly parents. I wonder what Jesus will say to those of us who will explain to Him that we were too busy with our careers, our ministries, our church activities, and vacations to see that our parents were cared for and honored? I pray I never find out.

Molly's Meatball Lesson #38

If you're too busy to care for and about your own parents,
you are too busy.

Pellegrino. But Not The Water

"Each of you must respect your mother and father."

— LEVITICUS 19:3

I never met my grandfather, Pellegrino Signoriello, but He was my mother's hero. If I base my assessment of him on her memories, he was as great a man as has ever lived. At least he was to my mom. She respected him in every way. He was part of a huge group of Italian-Americans who came to believe in the grace of God through the blood of Jesus rather than the rules and regulations of the religion they'd been raised in. Through my grandparents, and others like them, there was a real God-inspired revival in this group of immigrants who arrived in New York City in the first decades of the 20th century. So many people were born again and had become new creatures in Christ that Protestant churches popped up all over New York City filled with

Italian immigrants and their children and grandchildren. My grandfather became the founding pastor of a church in Staten Island that still exists and thrives today.

The stories my mother tells of my grandfather are always filled with his passion for Jesus, for people and about the miraculous power that comes from being devoted to God's Son. During the Great Depression, my grandfather had a job with the city of New York. It was a laborer's job. Incinerating trash. Still, it was steady work and income, so the family of seven children and my grandmother never did without the basic necessities. During this time, my mom and her sister visited a young friend of theirs and noticed they had no food. When they returned home, they told her dad. Immediately, my grandfather took the two of them by the hand, walked to the main street, hired a taxi, went to the grocery store, bought bags of food, and delivered it to these people. And he kept making sure they never did without food again. She tells story after story of observing her father do this kind of stuff.

Although he had a job, they weren't rich by any means. Still, on Sundays after church, the people would gather at my grandparents' home – their pastor and wife - for fellowship, and of course, for food. My grandparents generously put out any food they had. One Sunday night, when she was a young girl her father called to her and said, "Daughter, do you see the food that is on the table?" She nodded yes.

"When the people leave tonight tell me how much food is on the table."

And that night, when all the people were gone, and had eaten till they were full, my mom made note of the fact there was just as much food on the table as when the people had first arrived.

All through her life, her father lived a life worthy of the honor she gave him.

Molly's Meatball Lesson #39

Honor your father, especially if your father honors the Lord.

'Give Me A Kiss And Sleep In Peace'

"Do not despise your mother when she is old."

— Proverbs 23:22

The word *matriarch* was invented for my grandmother, Fiorina. We all loved and rotated around her. We called her Nonnon. My grandfather died of a heart attack while on the job in 1946. For the next 30 years, my grandmother was a widow who was well loved and taken care of by her family. And in an effort to give honor where honor is due, the reason my mother is a praying woman – and the reason you are reading about *her* – is because Nonnon was the original woman of prayer. She modeled a life of prayer for her whole family. "Ask Nonnon to pray" was my go-to response whenever something in my life needed prayer. I was not alone. The whole family depended on the prayers of our precious grandmother.

My childhood was filled with the understanding that prayer is a powerful weapon in the hands of a believing woman. Or man. When she died, my grandmother didn't leave us any money or material possessions but she taught my mother how to pray, and how to walk a walk of faith before God Himself. She left me the greatest inheritance I could ever have. I know how to pray. I'm a rich woman.

As I wrote in an earlier chapter, my grandmother found the Lord in a real and powerful way. As a result of her decision to open my grandfather's Bible one morning, everything about her life changed forever. My grandparents became His witnesses for Jesus. They didn't have evangelical traditions. So they didn't know any better than to simply read the Bible and do exactly what it said to do. As a result, many of their friends and family met Jesus in a real way, and not just a religious ritual kind of way.

In everyday ways, I saw what it meant to honor my Nonnon.

- **Speak with Honor.** I never heard my mom, any aunt or uncle, or any of my 12 cousins ever speak to Nonnon in a disrespectful way.

Ever. If someone might have been temporarily insane enough to be tempted to do so, the entire family would have come down on that person in a quick and forceful manner.

- **Honor Her by Listening.** When Nonnon spoke, the family listened. I saw my mom and her sisters and their husbands always defer to her when we were gathered together. What she said *mattered* to the family. Even if in our hearts we didn't care what she was talking about, we listened to her as if it were the only thing we cared about in the entire universe. I saw my mother honor her mother by listening to her in an honoring way.

- **Honor Her with Time.** The family regularly visited her home. As a young girl, my happiest memories are of being at her house, with my cousins, and aunts and uncles. Even as we grew up and moved away, we always came home to Nonnon. It was just always understood that being with Nonnon and caring for Nonnon was a joy and an honor. That was the attitude of heart I observed. Being with her mother was my mother's joy, not duty. It showed in her words, in her attitude, and in her time.

- **Honor Her Wishes.** Nonnon was a gentle giant. She was wise and never interfered in the lives of her sons and daughters – and their spouses - unless she saw that there was some kind of misunderstanding or division happening among family members. We had a happy and harmonious life with all our aunts, uncles and cousins. Nonnon would not tolerate any of her children having any kind of grudge against one another. She was relentless until she saw forgiveness given and received and peace restored to the family. A divided family – no matter the reason – was not allowed. And we honored her wishes and made up quickly during those moment we did not get along.

- **Honor Her by Caring about and for Her.** When she was older and needed care, Nonnon's daughters cared for her. She never did without one thing. She had little money but you'd never know it. The family took care of her needs. When Nonnon was older and couldn't be left alone at night, my mother and her four sisters took turns being at her home, sleeping overnight and just being with their mom.

(As I type this, I am sitting at my parents' house at 2:00 AM because they are 91 and 92 and shouldn't be left alone at night anymore. I didn't come up with this idea on my own. I saw my mom do it for her mom.)

Nonnon died peacefully in her sleep when she was 85 years old. Just hours before she passed, my mother called her before she went to bed. Mom said to her mom, "Give me a kiss and sleep in peace." (She said it in Italian). My mother heard the sound of her mother kissing her over the phone. And then the Lord Himself came and escorted my grandmother out of this world and into eternity. My mother still misses her mother. And I cannot imagine life without mine. I cannot imagine it.

Molly's Meatball Lesson #40

It's very likely that the way your treat your parents is the way your children will treat you.

Dishonorable Dads And Monster Moms

"Though my father and mother forsake me, the LORD *will receive me."*

— PSALM 27:10

It's easy to honor a father who raised me in a godly way and whose prayers were the background noise I heard when I fell asleep and night, and when I woke in the morning. It's an honor to honor a mother who so delighted in me that you'd think I was the only daughter ever born to any woman. But how does someone honor dishonorable parents? My mom used to counsel women that the first step is to forgive them. With some parents, this is easier said than done. It may take years, but forgiveness is still necessary for your own healing. You probably will need the support of others who love you and love God. You need the help of the Holy Spirit, your pastor, fellow Christians, and maybe a Christian counselor. My mother used to say, "If you really want to forgive someone, you really will. When God sees that real desire in your heart to forgive the unforgivable, that's all God really needs to see. He will give you the strength to do it." At the same time, Mom would cry with them, comfort them and be like a mom to them. She knew that some wounds heal slower than others.

Secondly, she would discourage a woman (or a man) from speaking publicly and disrespectfully about the parent who had hurt them. Of course, this is not the same thing as confiding in someone in order to heal inside. Keep their dishonor between you and God and a few people who are praying with you and for you.

My mom used to hug those women who didn't have moms who hugged them. She would say, "Your parents, or parent, may have been dishonorable, but your Father in heaven is the one who has seen it all. Give it to Him. Cast it on Him. You have a Heavenly Father and He has given you an eternal family."

Finally, my mom would always say that the best way to overcome having dishonorable parents is to be an honorable one. Be the kind of parent your child will be able to honor. Live a life that is pleasing to God, even if you didn't see your parents doing so.

Molly's Meatball Lesson #41

If you can't say something nice about your parents,
don't say anything at all.

EVERYDAY HONOR

When he was younger, my father was an expert jazz pianist. A really, really great pianist. I remember a snippet of conversation about when my dad was serving in the Army Air Forces during World War II. For a while he was a member of Glenn Miller's band. He was that good. I remember as a little girl that people were fascinated by his musical abilities. And one of the ways Mom taught me to practice every day honor toward my father was to not disturb him when he was playing the piano in our living room. "When Daddy is playing the piano," she cautioned, "leave him alone." Mom taught me that I was not the center of the family universe. I learned that my father was not created to pay attention to me all the time. I learned that my father was a person, a man, a husband who had a wife who loved him and who wanted him to have some time for himself. My father deserved to play the piano undisturbed.

I honor these two people who lived their lives for Jesus, who were the same way at home as they were in public. I watched them be honest and open in all their ways. I watched them love God with all they had and I felt them love me the same way. They deserve honor. I honor them.

Molly's Meatball Lesson #42

Honoring your parents is an everyday event. Do it every day.
And make it an event.

Honor Starts In The Heart

"Even small children are known by their actions."

— PROVERBS 20:11

My mother's godly wisdom and her recipe for living life started with the way she modeled honoring her parents. It wasn't just tradition and her desire to rule with an iron hand. She wasn't interested in subservience from me. She just required plain and simple obedience. It was the greatest gift and most fundamental recipe for living for me to understand that I was not running the universe, and that the universe never intended me to do so. As with all things, her basis for requiring this from me had its root in her reverence for God. God told us to honor our parents. So that's what my mother did. And that's what she expected me to do.

This helped me later in life when I gave my life to God. I understood that He's in charge and I'm not. When Christians end up being discouraged when God doesn't discuss His plans with them, I wonder if maybe they had parents who didn't teach them that a father's love means more than letting the kid get whatever the kids wants all the time. God is God. I am not. This is a fundamental element of humility and humility is the fundamental element of getting right with God. And getting right with God is the only thing that really matters. Really.

Molly's Meatball Lesson #43

A child who will blatantly disobey a parent will have no fear of blatantly disobeying God.

7

IF MARIE WAS A PRAYING WOMAN

The Recipe For Being A Wife

*"Follow God's example, therefore, as dearly loved children and walk
in the way
of love, just as Christ loved us and gave himself up for us as a
fragrant
offering and sacrifice to God."*

— EPHESIANS 5:1-2

My father was the king of our home, but I never observed my mother being anything other than his queen. As I write this, my parents' marriage
has flourished for over 72 years. They are hugging and kissing lovebirds
until this day. I never saw a husband vs. wife or a man vs. woman struggle
between my parents. They were not two people vying for control of their
marriage. They were one. They were on the same team. They lived the
Scripture: *"Submit to one another out of reverence for Christ"* (Eph. 5:21). They
spent more time trying to figure out how to please and serve each other
than trying to figure out how to have the upper hand in their marriage.
I know it sounds predictable and schmaltzy to say that, but it's the truth.

I grew up in the 1950's and 1960's. The world was different then. Men and women's roles have changed dramatically. Though the world has changed, marriage is still pretty much the same. It's a man and a woman who were convinced at some point in their past that their future would not be complete without one another. Marriage is still about weathering the storms of life together and soaking up the sun when skies are blue. It's still a man and a woman who are doing their best to raise their kids while paying the bills needed to raise them. Men and women haven't changed that much even in the middle of a role revolution on the earth. I saw in my parents' marriage that God intended marriage to be "The Garden of Eden" – not hell on earth.

I would like to share some things my mother taught me about being a wife. She taught me by example.

You may not agree with or like the way my mother did her life as a married woman. Some of her advice to me may not be the advice you want to include in to your life as a married woman. That's OK. She keeps telling me to be sure that I write that she and my father were not special or more spiritual than anyone. She wants to be sure I write that it is Jesus who accomplished anything good in their marriage and our home. (I told them, Mom. OK?) But if her example blesses you, encourages you and gives you hope that God can make every marriage whole and happy, then "Hooray and Hallelujah!" My parents are happy to be married to one another. Happy. Happy. Happy.

Molly's Meatball Lesson # 44

A miserable marriage is never God's idea.

Living "In The Same Way"

"Wives, in the same way submit yourselves to your own husbands."

— 1 PETER 3:1

Let's get the "submit" thing out of the way. I never heard my father demand it and I never saw my mother resist it. I was never told that when I got married I needed to be a submissive wife. I watched my strong and feisty and opinionated mother willingly give my father the respect and honor she knew would please God. And that's the key. Pleasing God was way more important to Molly Bruno than pleasing Joseph Bruno. Pleasing God was way more important to Molly Bruno than pleasing Molly Bruno. And as a result of her desire to please God, she pleased everyone around her. Surprisingly, rather than being a sour, sad, submissive robot of a woman, she is one of the happiest people I know. She is always laughing, always fun. Never discouraged. Never depressed. Honest.

She lived an "in the same way" kind of life about everything, including marriage. The verse above, 1 Peter 3:1, is a directive for followers of Jesus to live our lives "in the same way" Jesus lived His. Everything Jesus did, He did willingly. Every time He didn't answer back when someone insulted Him, every time He didn't demand His rights as the Son of God, every time He kept silent instead of lashing out about His innocence, He left us an example to follow. We all have God-given rights. Every woman has the right to choose to refuse to let her husband lead the marriage in the home. God gives every woman that right. If submission is not a woman's willing choice, then it isn't submission.

Jesus gave us that exact example with His own life. Jesus was not a martyr. He said, *"The reason my Father loves me is that I lay down my life—only to take it up again. No one takes it from me, but I lay it down of my own accord. I have authority to lay it down and authority to take it up again. This command I received from my Father"* (John 10:17-18).

Jesus gave Himself up for us. Jesus was not concerned when people treated Him unfairly because, *"He entrusted himself to him who judges justly"* (1 Pet. 2:23). He trusted His Heavenly Father to do the right thing for Him, and so did my mother. She trusted God completely. How do I know this? I saw her. I watched her. I observed her. She didn't retaliate. She didn't defend herself. She just trusted God. And God trusted her with her daughter and others: to teach them, love them, mentor and guide them.

Another verse says, *"Wives, submit yourselves to your own husbands as you do to the Lord"* (Eph. 5:22). I interpret this verse saying to me as a wife, "In the same way you are already submitting to the Lord, that's how you should submit yourself to your husband." If I'm not living a life of submission to the Lord, then I am going to have a major, big-time struggle to submit to my husband and to any authority in my life. Jesus gave Himself up for people who were not worthy of His sacrifice. He didn't say, "What? Me? The Son of God giving up My very life for this stinky, arrogant, stupid man?" Furthermore, He gave His life up for people who rejected Him, despised Him and crucified Him. In the same way, we don't submit **after** we see God being fair and just. We submit first and then, in time, we will see the justness of God. As Peter was advising the early church to submit to every authority, Christians were being killed for being Christians. Peter was not living under a just authority when he wrote those instructions. In the same way, many husbands are not the kind of husbands God expects and requires them to be. Sadly, and for reasons I cannot understand, many husbands are not being cautioned that the way they treat their wives has a direct connection between the way God responds to their prayers (1 Pet. 3:7). Really? Really. Prayer is an integral part of following Jesus and overcoming in this life on earth. If I were a husband, I would want to know that my prayers might be hindered because of the way I am treating my wife. But, that's between God and our husbands. We wives follow God's instructions anyway. We obey God anyway. And we entrust ourselves to "Him who judges justly." God defends us when we give our injustices to Him.

All day long, whether we realize it or not, we are submitting to authority. Like, for example, when we stop at red traffic lights. Most of us don't take the time to think to ourselves, "Wow. Look at me submitting to the highway authorities. Who do they think they are telling me I have to stop my car now because the light turned red?" No, we don't think that. We understand that when we stop at red lights, we are helping traffic to flow smoothly and safely. We understand that it isn't our slavery but our safety that makes the light turn red and requires us to "submit" to it. We submit to authority. Truth is that you and I have the human right to decide to not stop at red traffic lights. We don't have to put the brakes on. But, if we choose to ignore red traffic lights, we will cause damage to ourselves, our cars, and to others and their cars. So we stop. We submit. We protect yourself and others. And then we go on with your day. We don't accuse anyone of being unfair or of trying to rob us of our personhood by expecting us to submit to red lights. We stop. Then we go. That's it.

Mom taught me that I am called to respect God's authority to create authority on this earth. The earth is not a democracy. We did not elect God. He elected us to be forgiven and restored into His family. We are not running this planet, God is. And for some reason, known only to Him, God has decided that the husband gets the responsibility and the honor of being the head of the home. Why? I don't know why. He just did. Furthermore, He expects us to accept His decision by humbly acknowledging His absolute right to absolute authority.

God respects a woman's right to choose – or reject - submission. He doesn't force it. Submission isn't submission unless it is your choice. My mother just chose to do marriage the way God's Word explained it. No questions asked. And that was that.

Molly's Meatball Lesson #45

Two people who think they know how marriage works better than the One who created it are two people who don't know the One who created marriage.

Everyday Honor and Respect

"However, each one of you also must love his wife as he loves himself, and the wife must respect her husband."

— EPHESIANS 5:33

"Her husband is respected at the city gate."

— PROVERBS 31:23

As a woman and a wife, I really love Ephesians 5:33 because it reminds a husband that the way he loves himself is his pattern for loving his wife. I saw my father do this. I saw my father love my mother more than he loved himself. I have to give him the honor he deserves because he made it so easy for my mom to let him lead. He regarded her as a precious blessing in his life. That's not always the case for many wives. Some men expect submission without the "loving her as much as he loves himself" part. I am not advocating anything but obedience to God and His Word. I'm not making excuses for women who don't submit. I'm just explaining that some women don't feel the love. So then what should come first in a marriage – a submissive wife or a husband who loves her the way he loves himself? The answer to that can be found in a few other simple questions. What came first: Jesus laying down His life for the church or the church submitting to the lordship of Jesus? The answer is obvious. First, Jesus loved us. Then we loved Him back. I believe a husband is called to love unselfishly first. I think we misinterpret this. And what love truly is. Jesus is not the church's puppet, doing whatever we tell Him to do. Still, Jesus was willing to give up His life for us before we were willing to submit to Him. I think that's the pattern for a godly marriage. My father loved my mom first. And then I saw my mother honor and respect my father every day in everyday ways, including the following:

- **The way she spoke to him.** There was never exasperation, agitation, or aggravation in the tone of Mom's voice. I don't recall hearing her say anything to him in anger, nor do I recall an attempt to cause him pain with her words. I'm sure that there must have been moments when she wanted to hit him with a kitchen spatula, but I never knew it if she did. I never heard her call him a derogatory name. I never heard her point out a weakness he may have had. Every sentence I ever heard – let me repeat that – every sentence I ever heard her speak to him was covered in grace and love and respect and honor. The way we spoke to him was also expected to be with respect and honor. Having dinner together was the highlight of our day. And on some days, we had something to tell Daddy. Maybe we did something wrong, or maybe we needed his help to figure out something difficult. She told us, "Let Daddy eat dinner first. Let's eat dinner in peace. And then, when dinner is over, we will tell him what we need to tell him." Looking back, I see that this policy of not dumping our words on Daddy after he had worked a long, hard day was Mom's way of teaching us to honor him.

- **The way she spoke about him.** I'm sure that in 72 years of marriage, my parents hit some bumpy roads, but I don't know what they were, or where they hit them. Mere months after they were married, my father was stationed in England fighting in World War II. They didn't see each other for the first three and half years of their marriage. My father didn't see my brother until he was a toddler. I'm sure they must have had some adjustments in those early years of marriage. But I don't know about it. I just don't know any bad stuff about my dad because Mom never spoke anything about him that might have wounded her. I don't know if she was ever annoyed at him for small things like not picking up his socks or leaving the toilet seat up. I never knew if he snored too loud. I still don't know if he ever made any really stupid decisions. To this day, I don't know if anything about my dad has disappointed her, hurt her, wounded her or made her feel betrayed. I don't know about anything he might have done to break her heart. She loved my father. I saw in their lives that true love covers the other person. The Bible says it this way: "Above all, love each other deeply, because love covers over a multitude of sins" (1 Peter 4:8). It might seem natural to our wounded flesh to want to let everyone know when someone hurts us. It might be natural, but it isn't love. Love covers. Mom's respect for my father would never allow anyone to speak negatively about him, including her. Because of the way she spoke to and spoke about my father, my respect for him was off the charts.

Molly's Meatball Lesson #46

Your husband's reputation is formed by the words of your mouth.
Be careful with it.

- **She Never Complained.** About anything. I never heard her complain about how hard she worked or how no one appreciated all she did around the house. She never complained about other people, how they annoyed her or hurt her. I never heard her gossiping to my father about anyone and I never heard her say negative things about others. The more I have studied her and her life, I have come to understand that this control of her tongue blessed her life – and mine – greatly. I don't know who may have hurt her, betrayed her, used her or abused her. She just never complained about anything. Reminds me of the Scripture, *"Therefore if you have any encouragement from being united with Christ, if any comfort from his love, if any common sharing in the Spirit, if any tenderness and compassion, then make my joy complete by being like-minded, having the same love, being one in spirit and of one mind. Do nothing out of selfish ambition or vain conceit. Rather, in humility value others above yourselves, not looking to your own interests but each of you to the interests of the others.... Do everything without grumbling or arguing"* (Phil. 2:1-4; 14).
- **Living Within Their Budget.** On many marriage websites, you will find the surprising statistic that money is the subject couples argue about the most. Just do a search for "What do couples argue about most" and you'll find this to be true. My parents never did. Mom never once voiced a desire to have something they couldn't afford, or go somewhere they didn't have money to go. I never ever, ever heard her disparage my father because she was doing without something due to lack of money. She was thankful for what she had. She lived within their budget and that was that. My parents lived paycheck to paycheck. I knew this to be true because every Friday night my dad walked in the door with his paycheck. (For many years, he worked a full time job as well as

being a pastor.) They put the paycheck on the kitchen table and we would gather around, put our hands on the paycheck and thank God for giving us the blessing of my father's job. They prayed for wisdom in spending it. And that's the only time my mom and dad discussed finances in front of us. I never did without anything I wanted, but I was aware that my mother did her best to stretch a dollar. If she did without stuff and she resented doing without it, I never knew about it.

- **A Place For Everything And Everything In Its Place.** *"Everything should be done in a fitting and orderly way"* (1 Cor. 14:40). Those are the instructions Paul gave to the church in Corinth about how God's house should be run. My mother followed his advice about her house. Our home was a well-run entity. She made it clear by her attitude and actions that it was a high honor for her to create and keep order in our home. Children thrive in a well-ordered home. We knew where everything was. If we needed scissors, or a broom, or a paper and pencil, it was where she had predetermined to put it. And after we used it, we put it back where it belonged. I never wondered if the laundry would be done, if dinner would be cooked, if my blouses were be ironed. They just were. Looking back, I understand that her willingness to do the mundane created a foundation of security for all of us. My mother never wavered in her devotion to keep things running smoothly.
- **Number One Daddy – Not Number Two Mommy.** Because her life was different and she never worked outside the home, Mom has great respect for wives and mothers who work at a full time job outside the home. I cannot count the times I heard her praying for women as she spoke to them on the phone. Most of the time it was for God to give strength to these exhausted wives and mothers. She cried with them. She encouraged them. I also heard her fearlessly telling their husbands that if he is benefitting from her willingness to work at a full time job, "You need to help more around the house! You don't sit down at night and relax until your wife sits down and relaxes." Heaven help the husband

who didn't do what "Sister Molly" told him to do. She also cautioned these extremely exhausted women to avoid the temptation to treat their husbands as "Mommy Number 2". She didn't think it was wise for a woman to so focus on her children and their needs that she forgot about her husband and his needs. She didn't like the idea of a marriage being so child-focused that a husband and father simply became overworked Mom's extra set of hands. She's advised young wives, "For a season you need all the help your husband can give you. But make sure that season ends as the children grow. Make sure he is respected as the head of your home. Make sure he is always Number One Daddy and not Number Two Mommy."

Molly's Meatball Lesson #47

Don't let the kids take priority all the time. First you were a wife.
Every now and then take the time to keep first things first.

You might think that my parents were just two people who were fortunate to have a spouse who was easy to get along with. I don't think it was anything my father did or didn't do that caused Mom to be such a happy, contented woman. Early in my marriage, I got some insight into her secret weapon for wedded bliss. Prayer. Prayer. And more prayer.

"If Marie Was A Praying Woman"

"I love the LORD, for he heard my voice; he heard my cry for mercy.
Because he turned his ear to me, I will call on him as long as I live."

— PSALM 116:1-2

The year was 1971, I was 19 years old and I had been married for two years. Yes, I was only 17 years old when Phil and I were married 45 years ago. We'd dated all through high school. Our "dating" consisted of seeing each other at church, and maybe taking a ride on the Staten Island Ferry on a Saturday afternoon. I skipped two grades when I was in elementary school, so even though Phil is two years older than me, we both graduated from high school in 1968. Many, many people told us we were too young to get married. Most of those people are no longer alive. If they were alive, I'd tell them they were absolutely correct. We were too young to be married, but we didn't realize it at the time. We loved the Lord and we loved each other. He helped us whenever we cried out to Him for help. And we cried out to Him for help several times a day.

Another reason we got married so young can be traced to the Vietnam War. Right out of high school, Phil joined the Navy Reserve. His active duty was due to begin January of 1970. So we planned our December 1969 wedding for a year so we would be married before he left. As it turns out, he did not serve in a war zone, and we were able to be together for most of his deployment. When his two-year stint was over, we returned home to Staten Island. I was only 19 years old. He was 21. We were married babies.

One day we had a horrific, horrible, heinous argument. I don't remember about what. I just remember that I was convinced that Phil had done a terrible, horrible, no good thing. Phil, however, did not see the error of his ways no matter how diligently I pursued him with utter logic and incessant reasoning. We kept arguing and arguing. I was furious that he wouldn't apologize. Even more infuriating was the fact that he expected me to apologize. What? So, I took the situation to a higher power. I called Mom.

She answered the phone and knew immediately that I was boiling over with anger. She wouldn't allow me to talk to her about Phil unless Phil was on the other phone in our home. He reluctantly got on the other phone. It was not to please me, but to please my mom. He adored her. She listened to my explanation of what had happened. He was given equal time to rebut my diatribe about him. Because I know my mother, I sensed that she agreed with me. But she didn't say so. She said, "Marie, you should not have involved me in this argument." And then she said a sentence to Phil that so floored me, and so changed the course of my marriage that I can never thank her enough for saying it. She addressed Phil, "Phil, if Marie was a praying woman, she would give this situation to the Lord in prayer. I believe the Lord would speak to you and convict you about what you did. Now you two go get right with God and with one another. Quit this arguing." And with that she ended the conversation. That was the last time she allowed me to make her my Marriage Referee.

I was shocked that she knew I was not a praying woman. I had no idea it was so obvious. Evidently, a praying woman can recognize the lack of peace in a non-praying woman. At that time in my life, I wasn't devoted to prayer. Although I saw my mother's devotion to prayer throughout my childhood, I never understood until that moment that she used it as a powerful weapon in her marriage. It was the first time I saw my mother as a wife and not just my mother.

In that one instant, before I could even hang up the phone, it dawned on me that maybe the countless hours she spent in her room during my childhood, praying with the door closed, might have been her way of fighting for her marriage and fighting for her family. In one sentence she reminded me about what she had always taught me: "*Our struggle is not against flesh and blood, but against the rulers, against the authorities, against the powers of this dark world and against the spiritual forces of evil in the heavenly realms*" (Eph. 6:12). There is a thief trying to destroy my marriage, my life and me. He never quits in his attempts to see my utter annihilation. And yours. There is an unseen world at work in this world we see with our eyes. Who knows how many arguments between husbands and wives are instigated in the bowels of hell? God does. Prayer is my first line of defense because prayer is what God responds to.

Mom's sentence insulted me, except for the fact that is was utter truth. In the years that followed, she taught me that prayer about my marriage – and everything – was not my chance to whine about my husband to God. It was not an anger-fueled "Go get him, God!" kind of soliloquy. It was the simple act of humbling myself to acknowledge that I could not control an impossible situation. I cannot control my husband, even though I would like to. The kind of prayer my mother taught me to pray is a genuine agreement with God Himself to put the matter completely into His hands and under His control. I cannot count the times that Mom's sentence that day was the catalyst for me to pray, "God, I'm giving this to You. I cannot figure out what Phil is thinking, but you hear his thoughts. You know his heart. You know what to do. So deal with him. And deal with me. And help us both to honor You."

I discovered an almost instant and great reward from doing this. The moment I prayed, the moment I poured my broken heart out to God, the moment I gave all my anxiety to Him, in a deep and inner place inside me and my spirit, I just "knew" that He cared about me (1 Pet. 4:7). I knew that I had been utterly heard by Love Himself. I knew He was my loving Father, and I knew He was Phil's loving Father. No father likes to see his children angry at one another, especially not our Heavenly Father. He comforted me when I prayed even before the situation changed. I know now that my mother's life of prayer must have also brought instant peace to her heart. Being in God's presence cannot help but bring fullness of joy (Ps. 16:11).

Over the years, little by little, following Mom's advice to pray first and debate later, I saw God work things out in ways I could never imagine. I would pray about something, and keep praying about something, and keep putting that something on the altar before God. And in ways I could never have thought of myself, God took care of it. God did things in such a way that only He could get the glory for it. You can read thousands of books about marriage. You can listen to tens of thousands of sermons and attend 900 marriage seminars. You can call your pastor, your pastor's wife and a godly marriage counselor. These are all great tools to help a wife learn how to fight for her marriage. But I learned a secret from my mom that is so simple that most women brush it off as insignificant. I discovered that honest, heart-felt prayer is the most powerful tool any woman has to help her fight for her marriage and her family.

You might be struggling in your marriage right now. You might think your husband is cruel and unfeeling and unkind. You may have lost hope that anything can ever change. You don't have to believe me, but I can tell you that if you will simply and completely give the situation to God, if you will acknowledge He is your only hope, He will help you. He will help you. You may have to keep giving the situation to God; you may have to keep crying out to Him. But if you persevere, God will change things. What will He change? I don't know. When will He change it? I don't know. I just know that if you truly want God's will and God's ways, and if you tell Him so, He will work it out. If God is on your side, who would dare be against you?

Molly's Meatball Lesson #48

If you don't pray for your family, who will? Pray. Pray. And then pray some more.

Appearance Matters

"The Lord does not look at the things people look at. People look at the outward appearance, but the Lord looks at the heart."

— 1 SAMUEL 16:7

Mom has worn the same hairstyle for decades. A cute little layered cut that requires her to curl, tease and spray her hair. It also requires a "perm" every three months because her hair is bone straight. Since she moved to Tennessee 14 years ago, I have become her hairdresser. I cut her hair, style her hair, and give her those perms. I put the perm rods in her hair while my father watches in amusement. Every time I do, she says to him, "I'm doing this to look pretty for you, Honey. I'm doing this for you." And he usually says something like, "You always look beautiful to me."

Even at 92 years of age, my mother knows something that many women seem to forget: a man notices the way a woman looks. It's the way he is wired. God sees a woman's heart. Her husband, however, can only see her outward appearance. And a wife's outward appearance matters to her husband. Oh, yes it does. I have heard her tell young wives many, many times, "Your husband cares about your appearance more than he might be brave enough to tell you." And more than a few times, these same women came back to my mom in shock when they discussed it with their husbands and discovered that Mom was right. He does notice how you look. He does care about your appearance. He may not mention that to you because, well, because he wants to have peace on earth. But he notices how you look. Oh, yes he does.

Ouch. Yes, I know. That hurts. That kind of wisdom sounds foolish to women living in the 21st century. It seems like archaic advice. And that's what many women tell her. She won't back down, even in the face of women being outraged at her saying, "Don't neglect your appearance." She didn't mean look like a supermodel or don't accept the changes to your body that having children brings. She just means care about your appearance the way you cared at first. "What about him?" women protest. "My husband doesn't care about the way he looks!" She'd say, "You worry about you."

Sometimes women would become upset and confess to her "What's the use?" I've let myself go." Mom used to say, "Start today with how you are today. Look the best you can look today even if you don't come close to how you looked years ago. I'm not saying look better than you can. Look the best you can. And let your husband know that you care about the way you look to him. That might help him begin to care about the way he looks to you. You never know."

Should your appearance be the only thing that matters to your husband? Or course not. If you asked Mom if your husband should care more about your heart for God than about the way you look, she would say a resounding "Yes!" If you asked her if he should care more about the kind of mother you are to his children than the way you look, her answer would be a big and loud "Yes!" Should he care that you care about others? Yes. Should he care that you put up with his mother? Yes. Should he care that you sacrifice material things so as to not burden him? Yes. Should he care that you encourage him to follow his dreams? Yes. Should he care that you are interesting enough to continue to follow your dreams? Yes. Should he care that you are fun and happy? Yes. Should he care that you work outside the home when you'd rather be home? Yes, yes, yes. A thousand times yes. There are 900 million things that should matter to your husband more than your appearance. But Mom says, "Don't be foolish enough to think it doesn't matter to him at all."

Molly's Meatball Lesson #49

No woman ever ruined her marriage by taking time to look good for her husband.

"God, Grudges, and the Wives Who Have Them"

"In your anger do not sin. Do not let the sun go down while you are still angry, and do not give the devil a foothold."

— EPHESIANS 4:26-27

"Do not be quickly provoked in your spirit, for anger resides in the lap of fools."

— ECCLESIASTES 7:9

If Mom knew that I was letting anger stay in my heart – toward Phil or anyone – she would not let me rest until I forgave that person. She would ask me the same question, "Marie, what does the Bible call a person who holds on to anger?"

"A fool, Mom. It calls that person a fool."

"Do you want God to call you a fool, Marie?"

"No, Mom."

"Then get rid of that anger and lay down that grudge you are giving a home in your heart."

"Yes, Mom."

Holding a grudge, or being angry with another person for a long period of time is something Mom would crusades against. I often witness her being genuinely perplexed when another Christian brushes off the consequences of allowing themselves to be unforgiving toward another person. It was one of the great mysteries of life to her that a follower of Jesus thought He would overlook a grudge. I never saw lingering anger in our home. There was no such thing as my dad sleeping on the couch because they couldn't forgive each other.

One day, as she was teaching a group of women who attended the church my dad pastored, I heard her Mom, "Because I know some of you very well, I know that some of you have allowed your husband to become your enemy. He has done things to you that you feel are unforgiveable. So now you view him as your enemy. What does Jesus say about you and your enemies? She read, *"You have heard that it was said, 'Love your neighbor and hate your enemy.' But I tell you, love your enemies and pray for those who persecute you"* (Matt. 5:43-44). She reminded each of us that loving our husband and praying for him was still our course of action – even if he'd become our enemy. She asked us, "Do you understand that you are allowing your husband and what he has done to you to affect your relationship with God Himself? Is not forgiving your husband worth affecting your relationship with your heavenly Father?" She read, *"For if you forgive other people when they sin against you, your heavenly Father will also forgive you. But if you do not forgive others their sins, your Father will not forgive your sins"* (Matt. 6:14-15). We know the Lord has mercy, we know He longs to forgive. But He doesn't like it when people who don't deserve His mercy decide that other people don't deserve theirs. And neither does my mom.

Molly's Meatball Lesson # 50

A wife who is unwilling to forgive her husband's mistakes is making a bigger mistake than the mistake she is unwilling to forgive.

Would You Want To Come Home To You?

*"Better to live on a corner of the roof than share a house with a
quarrelsome wife. Better to live in a desert than with a quarrelsome
and nagging wife."*

— PROVERBS 21:9,19

Mom's favorite phrase about marriage is, "The wife sets the tone for
the home. Your attitude as a wife, Marie, will create the attitude and
atmosphere that is in your home. What kind of home do you want to
have? A happy home? An angry home? Examine yourself and ask yourself, 'Would I want to come home to me?' And tell yourself the truthful answer!" Her wisdom always reminded me that the only half of my
marriage that I can control is my half. I will answer to God for my life,
not my husband's life.

One of the most precious gifts my mother ever gave me was to never allow me to blame others for what was going on in my life. Including
my husband. Mom didn't teach me to ignore the obvious, or live a lie.
Her attitude was: "Not everyone is going to treat you like a princess,
Marie. That's life. That's people. Get over it. Jesus loves you even when
someone else despises you." Mom wanted me to be the kind of person
who could overlook what someone else was doing to me in an attempt
to see why God was allowing it to happen. It isn't always easy to take
that approach, but it is certainly worth it in the long run. No matter
what is happening, and who is doing it, God is allowing it. Nothing
touches me unless God allows it. She taught me to ask myself, "What is
God trying to teach me by allowing this in my life? Is there something
He is trying to dig out of my heart?" It is natural to blame others, but
it doesn't always help a person overcome the struggle. Her tough advice
was not easy to accept. Mom doesn't back down in telling every wife –
and every husband – to be the kind of person you would want to come
home to.

Molly's Meatball Lesson #51

_The world is filled with people who refuse to see themselves honestly.
Don't assume you aren't one of them._

LOVE AND MARRIAGE

_"Love is patient, love is kind. It does not envy, it does not boast, it
is not proud._
_It does not dishonor others, it is not self-seeking, it is not easily
angered,_
_it keeps no record of wrongs. Love does not delight in evil but rejoices
with the truth. It always protects, always trusts, always hopes,
always perseveres._
_Love never fails.... And now these three remain: faith, hope and
love._
But the greatest of these is love."

— _1 CORINTHIANS 13:4-8; 13_

Mom's standard for deciding if she was acting in a loving way had its basis in God's Word. To her, love was not love if it wasn't what God was describing as love. She taught me to use God's Word to deal with my attitudes. Most often I would have to admit that I was in need of the Holy Spirit to come and do an inside job on my heart. You may think you are a loving wife but does your definition of love match God's definition?

For example she had a message for each of the following wives:

The Easily Offended Wife

"Love... is not easily angered. It keeps no record of wrongs" (v. 5).

I feel sorry for the woman who comes to Mom with a laundry list of things her husband has done wrong. I see that wife hoping that tough Sister Molly is going to defend her and wallow with her in her whiny-ness. Nope.

Instead of commiserating with her about how horrible Mr. Husband is, I know that the easily offended wife is going to get "the question": "Is that love? Is that how love acts? Does God have a list of all the ways you have disappointed Him? Does He read it to you every time you make another mistake? And why are you so easily angered at your husband? Is that what love does? Does God get easily angered at you? Have you prayed about your own heart? Have you asked the Lord to give you love for your husband?" Ouch. Ouch. Ouch.

The White Lie Wife
"Love….. rejoices with the truth" (v. 6).

Love loves truth. Love rejoices and skips and laughs and applauds truth. A marriage must have truth if it is going to have love. My mom always taught the women in her church (and me, too) that those little white lies are not little or white. They are lies. She would say, "When you tell one lie, you have to tell 14 more to cover the one you just told." Lying about spending, or what you said to his mother, or what you said to your kids, or the neighbor is destructive. It is also manipulative. Do you forget to tell the whole story? Do you think that isn't deception? It is." And furthermore, she would say, "Your husband may not know you are not telling him the whole story, but your children do. You are teaching your children that lying is acceptable if it makes life easier." Mom said to one woman whose daughter was caught in a web of lies, "Don't wonder why your daughter just lied to you. She grew up seeing you lie. Ask her to forgive you for living a life of lying, stop doing it, and you'll see a change in her. And while you're at it, ask your husband to forgive you for all the deception you introduced into your relationship with all the lying you have done." The woman decided to follow my mother's advice, and sure enough, the relationship between her and her daughter was healed. And her husband's heart was so touched by her honesty that it opened a whole new level of connectedness between them. A lying wife is forfeiting the truth that love requires. You cannot have love if you do not have truth.

The Prison Warden Wife

"Love.... does not envy" (v. 4).

Mom reminds, "Your husband and the hours in your husband's day belong to God – not you. When you were first dating and he said, 'I'm playing basketball with my friends tonight', you did not say, 'Oh, no you are not playing basketball with your friends tonight!' No, you smiled because you realized you were not the time warden." You are living way above your pay grade if you think you have greater dibs on your husband's time than God does. Of course, Mom wasn't telling wives that their husbands could live the life of a single man and never come home and help around the house. And she also understood that when a couple is first married they don't have the responsibilities of children, mortgages and careers. My mom would caution many younger wives to open the prison door and let Mr. Husband free now and then. It isn't love to envy your husband's desire to spend some time with other people. He doesn't love you less just because he loves other people. She'd caution, "Don't be jealous of his desire to be with other people he loves. Love does not envy. He isn't being selfish to want a night of good, clean fun with his friends. He's being human." As I mentioned in a previous chapter, Mom made it a rule in our home that when my father was playing the piano – his major source of relaxing – we were not allowed to disturb him. This taught me that husbands and fathers are not abandoning their families just because, every now and then, they want to do something by themselves or with other people. Husbands are allowed to have hobbies, free time, and fun. Marriage should never be about envying your spouse's free time. Envy in a marriage kills love.

The Christian Princess Wife

"Love....is not self-seeking" (v. 5).

You've seen her. She is well-versed in every verse about husbands laying down their lives for their wives as Christ did. She expects to be the Bride of Christ someday. Before that day comes, however, she requires being treated like a princess. She expects her husband to be like Jesus – in a suit with great paying job; helping around the house and with the kids; never saying "no" to anything she asks for. My mom would remind the Christian Princess Wife that Jesus is not the church's puppet, waiting for the church to give Him His daily schedule. Mom was a champion for the husband who might be married to a woman who felt entitled to getting her own way all the time. I heard her repeat this verse hundreds of times when speaking to a Christian Princess Wife: *"The Son of God did not come to be served, but to serve"* (Matt. 20:28). She would say something like, "You are called to resemble Jesus. How can you be serving your husband when all you care about is how he serves you? You cannot." Ouch.

Overwhelmingly Overwhelmed

"When I am overwhelmed, you alone know the way I should turn."

— Psalm 142:3

Although Mom is uncompromising in her desire to have women look at themselves first and do what the Bible tells them to do, she is mostly filled with empathy and great compassion for wives and mothers. She understands the ups and downs of trying to do what needs to be done, and trying to do it successfully. So many women treat her as if she is their own mother because she treats them as if they are her daughters. You may be thinking about your life as a wife and mother, "I can't do this. Not for one more day." You may only see where you are failing and not anywhere you are succeeding. My mom would understand these feelings and remind you that God gives hope. Feelings of hopelessness are never His idea. My mom would tell you that you can do all things through Christ. She would remind you that He is right there. Right now. And don't feel guilty that you are not overcoming this overwhelming overwhelmingness. There is hope. Yes, there is.

Here are some things to think about:

1. Feeling overwhelmed is not a sign of weakness.

Sometimes life has seasons where things are just tough. This is how life is. The overwhelmed woman believes she is weak because life is overwhelming at the moment. Take heart. Even Jesus was overwhelmed in the garden when He realized what God was expecting of Him. Even though He was fully God, and He knew the reason He came was to conquer death, still He said, *"Father, take this away from me. I cannot drink this cup!"* (Matt. 26:42). Do you feel like you simply need the responsibilities to go away? Do you feel unqualified to care for the people in your care? Please find comfort in the fact that Jesus, above all others, understands what it feels like to see and know what God is requiring from you and being convinced that you are not able to drink that cup. It isn't a coincidence that when faced with the "cup," His response was prayer. He knew prayer would give Him the power to endure. Don't think He is disappointed in your weakness. He fully understands. Run to Him in prayer. Pour out your heart. He cares. He does. He does.

2. Feeling overwhelmed is the way godly people often feel.

I don't know where we got the idea that Christians need to act like we never have anything but overcoming thoughts. We certainly didn't get it from God's Word. The Bible paints a truthful story about the people God loves and cares for, and the people He uses to accomplish His plan. Feeling incompetent and insecure and inept is a common thread throughout the Old and New Testament. Remember Moses? He had the nerve to tell God Himself that He had made a big mistake, "I am sure you've got the wrong guy, Jehovah. Get someone else to deliver Your people." Ever feel like Moses? Do you ever think that God must have made a mistake when He decided to give you the husband and children you have? Do you feel inadequate to be what you need to be? Well, so did Moses. And look how God helped him to accomplish what He had in mind for Moses. God showed Moses He is the God who can split the Red Sea. Your impossible situation is nothing to the God who can split seas. And He is the God who showed Joshua that huge walls fall down through something as simple as praise. Take some time to simply thank God – out loud – for something. It could be for who He is. It could be for something you have. But praise Him out loud with your mouth. And what about Jonah, Ezekiel, Gideon, Hannah, David and Jeremiah? These great people of the Bible all had, "I can't do this anymore" moments. Peter? Paul? The Bible doesn't hide their overwhelmingly overwhelmed moments. As a matter of fact, most people in the Bible had severe doubts about their ability to figure life out. Most of them finally realized they couldn't figure life out and just fell upon the mercy of a loving God to guide them. You can do the same thing.

3. Feeling As If God Doesn't Care Is A Normal Reaction.

Sometimes life hits a person with wave after wave after wave, all at the same time. We don't feel like quoting Bible verses and praying prayers. We just want the storm to stop. We want the fear to stop. We want the waves to stop. But they don't stop. They keep getting worse. And it seems as if God is asleep, and when you pray you get His voicemail. The only thing more overwhelming than being overwhelmed is feeling like God doesn't care that you are. Well, join the group the Bible calls The Disciples. They were fishermen, used to storms, but were in "The Big One" and they were sure it was going to kill them. And they accused Jesus, saying, *"Don't you care if we drown?"* (Mark 4:38). Jesus stood up, said three words, *"Quiet. Be still"* (Mark 4:39). And the storm stopped. Their question was, *"Who is this Man that even the winds and waves obey Him?"* Although the disciples called Him in an accusing way – *"Don't you care if we drown?"* – He still calmed the sea for them. Jesus already knows what you are thinking: about Him, about life, about being a wife and a mother. You cannot hide your heart from Him. But when you call out to Him for help, He is right there. He will help you. The result of the storm in the disciples' life was that they saw the power of Jesus. Storms are sometimes allowed in our lives so that God can prove to us how powerful He is. If you feel as if you have lost your grip on God, if you feel as if you are just too weak, remember that He will never lose His grip on you. Being His follower is not about our ability to hold on to Him, but His power to hold on to us. You can't hold on any longer? Relax. He's got you. Until you come to the end of your own strength, you will never begin to comprehend the inexhaustible power of Jesus. He's got you. Relax.

Molly's Meatball Lesson #52

Storms are part of life on earth. In an instant, Jesus can calm every storm.

Family Focus

"Therefore, since we are surrounded by such a great cloud of witnesses, let us throw off everything that hinders and the sin that so easily entangles. And let us run with perseverance the race marked out for us, fixing our eyes on Jesus, the pioneer and perfecter of faith. For the joy set before him he endured the cross, scorning its shame, and sat down at the right hand of the throne of God. Consider him who endured such opposition from sinners, so that you will not grow weary and lose heart."

— HEBREWS 12:1-3

These are just a few of the things I learned from my mom about being a wife. Marriage has so many issues, and of course, I've just scratched the surface. In all things concerning her marriage, I saw my mother's focus be on Jesus. Her question went beyond, "What would Jesus do?" Her question came closer to "Who would Jesus be?" She wanted to be like Jesus. I saw my mother compare herself to His example. Every question we have, all the guidance we need, can be found in His example. Jesus considered that the end result of all His suffering would be joy. Whatever my mother had to lay down about herself in order to take up her cross and follow Jesus was worth the joy she had and that she passed on to her family. And to everyone she knew.

8

IF THE TIARA FITS...

The Recipe For Being A Mom

"The king's daughter is all glorious within: her clothing is of wrought gold."

— Psalm 45:13, KJV

When I was a child, I didn't notice what a great mother my mother was. I reasoned like a child, and just took her for granted. I assumed that a mom is supposed to make her daughter feel like the center of her universe. I didn't know that other daughters had moms whose universes did not revolve around them. I saw things dimly. Even now that we're both older, Mom continues to want to know me. She wants to understand me, to hear my heart, to listen to my stories, to let me pour out my frustrations on her and to share my joys. Her primary goal as a mom is to love me and to let me know she loves me more than she loves almost anything or anyone else on earth. Mission accomplished, Mom.

My childhood was a simple exercise of feeling secure and being firmly and lovingly guided in the path that I should go. And the path she wanted me to go is the Narrow Path (Matt. 7:13-14). More than anything else in the world, I was her "Jerusalem" and her major mission field. Of course she knew I had to choose the Narrow Path for myself, but she made it very clear that any other choice would be the wrong one. Her often repeated statement to me was, "Marie, if you wind up in China because that's God's will for your life and I never see you again while we both live on this earth, that's fine. I'd rather never see you again and know you are in the center of God's will for your life, than to have you live right next door to me and be out of the will of God." That was a great big statement for her to make because she liked me being close to her all the time. I liked being close to her too. She followed the advice Moses gave the Israelites as they were about to enter the promised land. He reminded these people that their children had not seen the miracles they had seen and that it was up to them to be sure their children knew the God they served and the commandments He had given them. He said, *"Teach them to your children, talking about them when you sit at home and when you walk along the road, when you lie down and when you get up"* (Deut. 11:19). This was the way my life was as a child. All day, every day, everything had a connection to God, His ways, His will and His love. Mom talked about Jesus constantly. She talked about what she'd read in the Bible that morning, and asked me what verse I'd read in mine. Her first response in every situation was to include Jesus – what He would do, what He would say, what He would want – and to include Him first. We prayed for wisdom or we prayed to give thanks. But in almost everything that happened, we prayed. Something as insignificant as finding a new dress I loved and we thanked Jesus for allowing me to have it. When I got a good grade at school, we thanked Jesus for allowing me to get it. When I was upset or distressed about anything, she would remind me that I could give my cares to Jesus. And as a little girl, that's exactly what I did. And He took them. As a child I could sense His involvement in every aspect of my everyday life. Because of this He was real to me. It's like He was sitting in our house, being part of our family.

When I was eight years old I gave my life to Jesus. I wanted Him to be the Lord of my life. I was baptized in water and filled with His Spirit. But ten years later, at eighteen years of age, I had a heart-to-heart talk with

Him. I was married and away from home. I was living where Phil was stationed for his military service. One day, I just poured my heart out to the Lord. I wanted more of Him in my life than simply going to church, volunteering at church and memorizing God's Word. I wanted a deep and real and vibrant relationship with Him. The only way I could explain what was in my innermost heart was to tell Him, "I want to love You the way my mother loves you. I want to love You with all my heart. I want to love You the way my mother loves You, Lord. Will You help me to love You that way?" That's the example she modeled for me: being head over heels in love with God. And His Only Son.

Because of how she lived her life, she didn't need to remind me that loving God meant loving others. I watched her live a life of serving God's people and putting their needs above her own. She made sure I understood that because I was the daughter of the King of the Universe, I was set apart from the rest of the world. I was chosen. I was a princess in the only Kingdom that will never end. *"But you are a chosen people, a royal priesthood, a holy nation, God's special possession, that you may declare the praises of him who called you out of darkness into his wonderful light"* (1 Pet. 2:9).

And Then "Glorious" Arrived

In 1974, I had been married for almost five years when our only child was born. My husband and I lived near Harrisburg, Pennsylvania, and my parents still lived in Staten Island, N.Y. I called my parents at 5 AM one morning to tell them I was on my way to the hospital to give birth. Soon after, they were on the highway to begin the three-hour drive to the hospital. We didn't know if we were having a boy or a girl. Whatever it happened to be, my mother knew it would be "glorious" because as she drove, she opened her Bible to the verse listed above (Ps. 45:13). She took it to be talking about what was happening to me as she drove to be with me. You'll notice the verse refers to "the King's daughter" being all "glorious within." That I was the King's daughter went without saying. Over the years, she would repeat this verse to my son, reminding him that he was the "glorious within." Every now and then she would actually call him "Glorious." She wasn't concerned about the accurate theological meaning of the verse. To mom, God was telling her that I was the King's Daughter giving birth to a glorious son. And there you have it: Molly Mothering 101. She had no problem making the whole family feel like the holy royalty we are. If the tiara fits – and it does – wear it.

Molly's Meatball Lesson #53

Remind your children of the eternal and royal identity every Christian possesses.
Jesus wore a crown of thorns so that His children could wear crowns of gold.

Sometimes "Love" Is A Two-Letter Word

"All you need to say is simply 'Yes' or 'No.'"

— MATTHEW 5:37

Mom made it clear to me that choosing to be a follower of Jesus meant choosing a path most people would not seek to find. She never tried to hide the cost of being a disciple of Jesus or the way it would mark me as different. She knew she was encouraging me to live a life of taking up my cross, denying myself, and following Him and Him alone. As a mother, she adhered to a stringent and restrictive policy concerning who and what she allowed into my life. She had no problem saying the word no. If I wanted to go somewhere and she didn't think it would be edifying for me to go there, she said no and that was that. We didn't reason it out or debate about it. After she said no, I never, ever changed her mind, although I often tried. I didn't see her reevaluating her decision or feeling bad about making it. No meant no. She was Mom and I was not. As I grew in to a teenager, Mom would offer this slight explanation: "I have to answer to God for the things I allow. I'd rather have you annoyed at me than to displease God by allowing you to do something

I know isn't good for you. You are His daughter and I am responsible to God for how I raise you."

Mom's "No means No" policy never bothered me until I was a sophomore in high school. My school had thousands of students and most of the girls in my grade already had boyfriends. I did not. My parents' idea about me having a boyfriend was strict and non-negotiable: I did not have a right to have a boyfriend. It was a privilege they would decide to let me have when they decided to let me have it. And Part B: When they did allow a boyfriend in to my life, he had to be a Christian in every sense of the word. To my parents, this meant, devoted to Christ. Following Christ. Being truly "born again."

I clearly knew and understood that this was their dating policy on that Tuesday in 1967 when "Tom" (name changed) showed up at my high school's cafeteria dressed in his Army uniform. Each lunch period at my school accommodated 600-700 students at a time. Tom had graduated the year earlier. The Vietnam War caused him to be drafted right out of high school. He was one of the "most popular" kids in school the previous year. He was a star football player and well-liked by teachers and students. On this Tuesday afternoon I was a junior - in 11th grade - I was fourteen years old. I had never spoken to Tom as far as I could remember. The year before, he had been a sensational senior and I was a shy sophomore. On this particular day I was sitting there in the cafeteria with my friends, minding my own business and eating lunch. Suddenly there was a wave of applause and excitement as Tom walked in to the cafeteria, looking handsome in his Army uniform. Lots of students ran over to greet him. I did not. Mainly because I didn't know him, and even if I did, eating lunch was an important moment in my school day. Tom had a steadfast look in his eyes. He looked around the cafeteria. It was obvious he was there on a mission. Lo and behold, his mission was to find me. All 600 students followed Tom's path to my lunch table and to me. He kneeled down next to me and said, "I've always wanted to get to know you, Marie." (Tom knew my name? I felt like I was going to faint.) He said he was home on leave, and wanted to know if I would go to our school's basketball game with him on Saturday night. Everyone was looking at me. I wanted to say

"Yes! Yes! Yes!" I wanted to go to the game with Tom. As he spoke to me, my reputation at school was being elevated as high as a cheerleader's. I was in a fog, but my brain was clear enough to remember Mom. I had to get her to approve this date. So my answer to his invitation was, "What church do you attend?"

"What?" his face looked confused.

"What church do you go to?"

"Uh, sometimes I go to the Methodist church."

"OK. Give me your phone number. I have to check with my parents. I'll call you tonight and let you know." He wrote his number down, and left the cafeteria.

All day that day I was a great big deal at school. All my friends treated me like I was a celebrity and the luckiest girl alive. I felt like the luckiest girl alive. Even some students who didn't know me stopped me in the hallway, "Did Tom ask you out on a date?"

"Yes he did." I was flying high.

After dinner that night, I brought up Tom's invitation. "Mom, Dad, there's this guy who graduated last year named Tom. He's really nice. He came to school today and asked if I could sit next to him at the basketball game this Saturday night." I didn't call it a date but Mom was no fool.

"Is he a Christian?"

"Well, he goes to the Methodist church."

"Yes, but does he love Jesus? Is he a Christian?"

Her line of questioning continued and my vague answers made it obvious that I had no idea who Tom was and what he was really like. As a result, Tom was not a candidate to be spending a night at a basketball game with her daughter that Saturday night or any Saturday night in the future.

"No!" she said.

"MOM! MOM! MOM??? Please let me go. You could drive me and pick me up. Please? Please. I really want to be there. PLEEEEEEZE Mom!!"

"No." And she gave me the "this discussion is over" look. And right after she gave me that look, the discussion was over.

I was very, very angry with Molly Bruno. I worked up my nerve and called Tom to say that I wasn't allowed to go out with him on Saturday.

He didn't like my answer. "I want to date you", he said, "I always have." This information was too much for me to bear. I could have been Tom's girlfriend? This would make me a very important student.

The next day at school everyone was making fun of me because I wasn't allowed to go on a date with Tom. For the first time in my life, a seed of bitterness about my mother and her strict policies found its way in to my childish heart.

On Saturday night instead of being at a basketball game with Tom, instead of being a popular girl with everyone at school because I was sitting there with Tom, instead of taking the first and necessary step to becoming "Tom's girlfriend," I was in the back seat of my parents' car on our way to – drum roll - a Youth Rally (a church service) in Bayside, Queens. All during the 40-minute drive on the Belt Parkway I was silently seething at my mother. I thought, "This is such a 'cool' youth meeting that my parents are going to it!" As it turns out, we were not the only people who lived on Staten Island who had taken the time to drive to this youth rally in Queens. A young and energetic pastor, Daniel Mercaldo, who had opened a new church on Staten Island a few years earlier was there as the guest speaker. He had formed a gospel music singing trio with two teenaged brothers who attended his church. They were singing when we walked in. I must admit I thought the two brothers were cute. Very cute. The older brother was standing behind a microphone next to the pastor, and the younger brother was sitting at the piano playing and singing at once. The trio was really good. Their music was great. The pastor was a great communicator. I enjoyed the entire meeting.

After the meeting, the piano player made a beeline to my side. He already knew my older brother Nick, who was a popular piano player with some well-known Southern Gospel groups. Evidently, at some point in the past, Nick had been kind enough to spend some time with this piano-playing kid at a concert or two. He'd taken the time to teach him some tricks on the piano. Nick was a hero to him. I was standing at the back of the church, and the piano player walked up to me and said, "Hi. Aren't you Nicky Bruno's little sister?"

And that's the night I met Phil Armenia for the first time. I had no idea I had just met my future husband. I had no idea that someday Pastor Mercaldo would become my pastor too. As my parents and I drove home that night, I smugly said to my mother, "That guy Phil likes me. He is for sure going to call and ask me out on a date. So, can I say yes when **he** calls?"

"Of course you can."

"Really, Mom?"

Really. The next Saturday morning, Phil Armenia called and asked me if I would go to a church Valentine's Day banquet where trio was performing. And I immediately answered, "Sure!" And the rest, as they say, is history.

I have often wondered what my life would have looked like if my mother had allowed me to go to a basketball game with some guy named Tom, instead of standing her ground and saying no. Thankfully, I will never know.

I learned a great big lesson from my mom. As a parent, sometimes love is a two-letter word – no.

Molly's Meatball Lesson #54

Don't say no all the time, but say it without hesitating when no is the right thing to say to your child.

Never Let Her Get To 3

"Do not withhold discipline from a child."

— PROVERBS 23:13

I don't recall ever getting a spanking or being slapped or being pushed or shaken or any physical correction by either parent. Oh, wait. That's not true. I remember one time when I was about four years old that my father spanked my bottom for something. But other than that, I never got a spanking. It's not because I was an angel child but because my mother was very diligent about keeping her word when she warned me about something. My mom always used the 1, 2, 3 disciplinary method. If I was doing something, or refusing to do something, she would simply and calmly say, "1, 2, 3." I knew that if my behavior did not change by the time she said 3, I would be in trouble. So my only way to avoid her displeasure was to never let her get to 3. Evidently, she had established a precedent for being diligent about meaning what she said and saying what she meant. There was a deeply imbedded reality somewhere in my inner psyche that knew she meant business when she started to say "1, 2, ..." I rarely heard "3" because my Momma didn't raise no fool. Here's some other simple stuff I observed about her mothering method that I tried to incorporate in to mine:

- **"Anthony Get Over Here or I'll Break Your Legs"** ...was a threat my mom and I heard a mother issue to her very unruly and out of control son one day when we were at the grocery store one day. She also told Anthony that if he didn't obey, she was going to break his arms or give him away to the police. I was about 14 years old. My mother used the opportunity to point out to me that "Anthony," who seemed to be about five years old, knew that his mother was not going to break his legs. Or break his arms. Or give him away to the police. Therefore her threats of punishment did not carry any power over Anthony, the tyrant kid. My mother said, "If his mother would have used an honest sentence, Anthony would be listening." She gave me examples like, "Anthony get back in the seat of this cart or you will not be able to eat the cookies we just bought." Mom was sure that Anthony wanted those cookies. She said, "But it isn't enough to have a more realistic discipline if you don't' carry through and do it." She taught me that a mom has to say what she means and mean what she says. So first rule of mothering is this: "Don't say something you know you don't mean and won't do." And if you say you are going to do something, then do it. You don't have to look far to see lazy parents who tell their children that there will be consequences for disobedience, but there never actually is. Just this week, I observed the parents of two boys we were visiting. At least five times the boys went outside and near their swimming pool – which was not allowed. At least five times I heard their Mom say, "Boys, if you go near the pool again, you can't play any video games today as your discipline." Each time she said that, the boys went by the pool. I think it was at least four more times. Each time she simply repeated, "Boys I told you not to go near the pool. You won't be able to play your video games if you go there one more time." Three times later, she said the same thing. The boys then walked in to the next room, picked up their video game remote and played for hours. Evidently, as long as they were quiet, Mom didn't care about following through on her words. But Mom's wisdom was, "Never break a promise to a child." And to her, that included whatever you promised as a reward or whatever you promised as discipline. She said to parents, "Don't issue threats that you and your child know you will not and cannot carry through." Evidently, before I was old enough to remember, my mom made it clear to me that it was in my best interest to never let her say "3."

Molly's Meatball Lesson #55

When disciplining your children, use your "or else"
sentences sparingly.
The only thing worse than your child not obeying you is you not doing
what you said you would do if your child did not obey.

- **Don't Exasperate Your Children.** "*Fathers, do not exasperate your children; instead, bring them up in the training and instruction of the Lord*" (Eph. 6:4). Although I lived with the knowledge that Mom (and Dad) had ultimate authority in my life, I never felt like I was being treated unfairly or that they were mean. (Well, except for a few days during "The Tom Incident"). The verse about not exasperating your children is one my mom quoted often. It seems to be saying that a parent can be mean-spirited and use the authority they have in such a way that it incites anger in the heart of the child. Don't throw your authority around like a big parenting bully. My paraphrase is, "Don't use your God-given authority so unfairly that you are the one who creates an anger in your child that is somewhat justified." So what should a parent do instead of exasperating their child? *"Bring them up in the training and instruction of the Lord"* is what the verse says. That's what my mom did. That's what my parents did. She never drew a line in the sand just because she could. She didn't make rules just to make rules. Her discipline had a deeper purpose – to do her best to keep my life in obedience to God's Word and not just because she felt like making rules.

Molly's Meatball Lesson #56

God never uses His power and authority to exasperate His children.
He isn't really happy with parents who do.

"Where Ever He Is, Lord, Bless Him."

I must have been just seven or eight years old the first time I remember hearing Mom pray, "Father, where ever he is right now, I pray for Marie's future husband. I pray that if he doesn't know You, Lord, he will come to know You. I pray that if he is sick now, that You will heal him. I pray that if he is afraid, You will comfort him. If he is in need, you will supply. Where ever he is, Lord, bless him. Take care of him, Lord. We love him already." I started praying for my husband before I even knew him and while I was still trying to get the hang of using a hoola-hoop.

As it turns out, Phil's family did not know the Lord. His father had gone to church as a child, but the family was not a Christian one.

When Phil was 12 years old, his father decided to take his family to the last night of a revival meeting at a church nearby. The evangelist's name was George Butrin. As the invitation to accept Christ was given, Phil's mom, his sister, his brother and Phil walked forward to receive Christ. The whole family gave their lives to Jesus that day. My mom had no way of knowing that "Marie's future husband" had just asked to be forgiven of his sin and to have a new heart. Before that moment, he was at a turning point in his life. He was beginning to get into small trouble here and there. George Butrin's message was the one that got to that young boy's heart – and that young boy's family. Years later, George's son, John and his wife Gayle became two of our closest friends. Imagine John's joy to know that his friend Phil would be in heaven forever with him and it was because of his father's life. Years later, my father became the associate pastor of the very church where Phil gave his life to the Lord.

I have often wondered if it was God's answer to my mother's prayers for Phil that was the reason my father-in-law decided to go to church that night. We'll know when we all get to heaven. When my son was growing up, I followed my mom's example and prayed for my daughter-in-law, Renee. And now I am praying for my grandchildren's spouses – wherever they are.

Molly's Meatball Lesson #57

If you want your child to marry a believer, it's never too soon to pray for and about their future spouse. And get your children to pray for them too.

Artichokes and Other Loving Objects

My adult journey toward knowing and appreciating my incredible mother began with an artichoke. Yes, an artichoke. My mom made a great big deal about having dinner together every night. Each day, at 5:30 PM, we had a full home-cooked meal. We sat down together, we ate together and we talked together. (She wants me to remind every wife and mother who works outside the home to not feel bad about not having time to cook a home-cooked meal for the family. But she says, "Tell them to be sure to eat together as a family as often as they can. Even if it's take-out, eat it together. Talk to one another. Turn off the phones and the texting." I told them, Mom).

Back to the artichoke story. Every now and then, my mom would announce that we were having artichokes for dinner. This announcement made me almost euphoric. I mean, anyone can heat up a can of peas, carrots, string beans or corn and place them on a plate. You pick up the spoon, eat them and that's the end of the vegetable adventure. Ho, hum. Oh, but not an artichoke. It's like a mystery vegetable. You have to peel it away, one leaf at a time until you hit the prize – the artichoke heart. I adored the process. Mom would season them in such a way that each leaf was filled with her mouth-watering seasonings. I always gave the artichoke heart to my mom. She told me it was the best part and would say, "Thank you for giving me your heart" and wink at me. I knew she meant the heart that loved her and not the mushy one inside the artichoke. I thought she was so cool for that double-meaning sentence.

When I was first married and still just a teenager, one of the first recipes I asked for was her artichoke recipe. She told me what to do, how to season them, cutting up some small little garlic pieces, and drizzling olive oil over the top and then add some Romano cheese. Just typing her recipe is making my mouth water.

I went to the supermarket to buy the artichokes. I was stunned at how expensive an artichoke is. I mean, really, you can buy a week's worth of canned peas for the same amount you spend on one single artichoke. Who knew that my mom was busting her grocery budget just to appease my constant begging for artichokes? She always did her best to give me what I desired. In an instant, in front of the produce section of that grocery store, I understood that I didn't understand how much it cost her to give me the things I asked for. She never mentioned that I was asking for more than they could afford. Not once. I couldn't afford a bowl full of artichokes like my mom used to put on the table, but I did buy four.

When I got home and took a closer look at the artichokes I'd purchased, it was obvious I didn't buy the kind my mother used to make. These odd little artichokes I'd purchased had sharp thorns on the end of each leaf. I don't remember thorns on artichokes. Who would want to eat something that has a weapon of mass destruction on the end of each leaf? Not me. Those thorns were nasty. I wasn't going near them.

I called her to let her know about my mistake. She said, "No, you got the right kind. I always used a scissor to cut the thorns off the end of the leaves before I cooked them."

"Mom, you took the time to cut every leaf on every artichoke you ever made?"

"Anything for my little girl."

Indeed. It got me wondering about how many other "thorns" of life my mother protected me from. It got just a glimpse into the way my mom protected me from pain whenever she could. She protected me. She surrounded me. She cushioned me. As long as I was living in her home, she cut the "thorns" off things before I got near them. She knew there was no way she could protect me from every thorn for all of my life but she tried. She really tried. Thanks, Mom.

Molly's Meatball Lesson # 58

Let God decide when and how your child needs to endure the thorns of life.
As a parent, do your best to remove the thorns you are able to.

"How I Prayed For You"

"May she who gave you birth be joyful!"

— PROVERBS 23:25

For most of my life, including right up to the present, my mother frequently reminds me that she prayed for me before my birth. That she wanted me very, very much. She explains that she became a little concerned that she wouldn't be able to have me as she was raising my brother. She wanted a daughter. So she prayed and prayed and prayed specifically for a little girl. After just a few months she found out she was expecting again. All my life Mom reminded me how much I was wanted. She said to me on several million occasions, "How I prayed for you. I prayed for you." I never really understood how much security and self-worth that knowledge instilled into the deepest part of my being until I grew up. Mom tells me that when my father saw me, he called everyone in the family to explode with the news, "She looks just like me!" (I do look just like my father.) She says my eight-year-old brother was thrilled too. (I'm not sure about the accuracy of that statement). All my life, the story I heard about my parents' reaction to my birth is that I was wanted, and prayed for, and cherished and rejoiced over. All my life my mother was joyful that I existed. Just because I breathed air brought her great joy.

Which brings me to something I heard her teaching with great gusto to the moms who were in her spiritual care. She would ask some very pointed questions like: "Why did you tell your child he was a mistake? Do you realize that God creates life? Does God make mistakes? What better way to make that kid feel unwanted than telling that kid he was unwanted?" This was a big parenting deal to my mother. It may not seem like a great big deal to many people, but try telling that to the person who went through life knowing he was "an accident." Mom would often repeat this sentence, "If you have already made the mistake of telling your child he was a mistake, then you cannot take those words back. But you can add words that will help toward healing. Tell him that it was a mistake to tell him he was a mistake because he is the best thing that ever happened to you. Every child is a gift from God. It is God who creates life. Who has to audacity to tell God His gift is a mistake? His gift is an accident?" Those are great questions, Mom. Great questions.

Molly's Meatball Lesson #59

*The biggest mistake a parent can make is telling
your child he was a mistake. Don't do it.*

Perfect In Every Way

*"Do not let any unwholesome talk come out of your mouths,
but only what is helpful for building others up according to
their needs, that it may benefit those who listen."*

— EPHESIANS 4:29

It seems to me that my mother learned very early in life that the most loving way to show your love is in the way you use — or don't use — your words. The words "unwholesome talk" in the Ephesians 4:29 means more than "don't use four letter curse words." An expanded definition of the word "unwholesome" is "rotten, corrupted, no longer fit for use, worn out, poor quality, bad, unfit for use, worthless"(Strong's). A word doesn't have to be a curse word for it to be unwholesome. It could simply be a rotten thing to say such as, "You're just like your lazy father" or a worthless thing to say such as, "You're never going to amount to anything!" It could be a worn out sentence like, "Dear God, please help me deal with these annoying children" or a poor quality sentence like, "We're poor. Get used to it." Tragically, these are actual sentences that actual moms have actually uttered to their actual children that I have actually heard. Epheisans 4:29 begins with telling us how we should not talk, and ends with telling us how we should: **only** what is helpful for building others up, **according to their needs.** My mother found the way to tell me what I needed to hear when I needed to hear it. If I needed encouragement, that's what she spoke. If I needed correction, that's what she spoke. If I needed spiritual exhortation, that's what I heard. The key is that she knew me. She spent time knowing who I was, what kind of heart I have and what it needed at the moment. Her words always reinforced her love.

Gracious Words

"Gracious words promote instruction. Gracious words
are a honeycomb,
sweet to the soul and healing to the bones."

— PROVERBS *16:21; 24*

I mentioned in the last chapter about the way my mother spoke to and about my dad. She did the same thing with me. She spoke gracious words to me. She instructed me with gracious words. She would tell me what was good about something instead of pointing out what was bad. For example, if she didn't like the way I was fixing my hair, she would wait until the day I fixed it differently and in a style she liked. She would say, "Oh, I really love the way you fixed your hair today. It's pulled back off your face and you can see your beautiful eyes and your gorgeous skin. You should always wear it this way." Those gracious words instructed me more than if she had said something like, "Why are you fixing your hair in that ridiculous style?" As I reflect back on my life, I see that her gracious words surrounded me in every way. Mom's example taught me that a mom should think about and consider the following:

- **The Way She Speaks To Her Children.** I want to be sure you get the accurate and complete picture of the Molly/Marie, Mother/Daughter relationship. I wouldn't want you to imagine the two of us walking around the house quoting Bible verses all day and singing sweet songs of heavenly harmony. We are a normal mother and daughter. Both of us are highly opinionated, talkative, strong-willed women. We are two New York Italian-American women. And I say that without fear of you stereotyping us. Stereotype to your heart's content. We **are** the stereotype and proud of it. We are direct and unedited and animated and passionate in the way we speak to one another. We don't always agree, but we don't expect to always agree. We make each other laugh, and we are both sort of irreverent. For example, as she has been aging, her days of public speaking and teaching Bible studies to women have drawn to a close. She lovingly said to me a short while ago, "My mantle is on you now, Marie." Meaning her "mantle of ministry." Rather than simply letting her words rest and being thankful for her motherly ordination, I answered, "Ma, what are you, Elijah?" (1 Kings 19:19). She laughed and repeated her sentence. My response didn't offend her. That's who we are. Love is not easily offended. We love each other. And yet, in spite of our direct and sometimes blunt communication style, she never said one angry, hurtful word to me in all my six decades of living on this planet. Now let me draw attention to the miracle that is Molly by repeating that sentence. She never said one angry, hurtful word to me. I am just as amazed at her self-control. I have seen other women who have had the privilege of being mentored by her try to be that way from the outside in. They soon discovered that no person could be that self-disciplined all the time just by using human will power. My mom's prayer was that the Holy Spirit would do His work inside her. That He would change her from the inside out. She spoke with love because love was living in her heart. She spoke with wisdom because the Holy Spirit gave it to her. She had kindness because she allowed the Holy Spirit to cultivate it inside her. My father used to teach me an important lesson using a drinking glass. He'd point out that when you bump up against a glass, whatever that glass if full of is what will spill out. So, if a mom is full of resentment instead of love, when something goes wrong in her day, the first thing that will spill out is resentment. If she is full of anger, that's what will spill out when life bumps up against her. But when life bumped up against my mom, love poured out. Contentment poured out. Kindness poured out. Wisdom poured out. Everything that Jesus is poured out. My mom never spoke to me in anger. That's not the same as saying she has never said something that hurt me. Sometimes when speaking the truth to me in love, it hurt. Sometimes I didn't want to hear what she had to say, and wasn't willing to let her voice an opinion about something. However, she was never so out of control in her spirit that she said something to me in anger just to hurt me. I never heard a sentence like, "You are so stubborn!" or "You drive me crazy!" or "Get out of my sight. Leave me alone, please!" Never. I have heard other mothers say these things to their children. I have done my best to never speak like that to my son. (You'll have to ask him if I succeeded.) I never knew if my existence had altered her plans for her life. I never knew if she was doing without something in order for me to have something. I didn't know what she thought were my weaknesses. I still don't. I didn't know what she thought was less than excellent about me. I still don't. I always knew she thought I could do all things through Christ. I always just assumed that when I came along, I made her life perfect in every way.

Molly's Meatball Lesson #60

Our Heavenly Father never makes us feel like He sacrificed too much in order to have us as His child. Don't ever make your child feel like you have sacrificed too much to be a parent.

- **The Way She Speaks About Her Children.** "*Does not the ear test words as the tongue tastes food?*" (Pro. 12:11). Mom has always been a champion for the tender hearts of children. Her words **about me** to other people were always good words, proud and excellent words. To this day, if you get close to her for more than five minutes she will tell you that I am a writer, and I write songs, I sing beautifully, and I teach the Bible to women. If you judged by what she says **about me,** you would be convinced that I write the best articles in any magazine, that my songs are the best songs ever written since the beginning of time, that my voice is the voice of an angel and that I am the best Bible teacher God ever created. She is very biased, obviously. But that is what she says about me to others. That's her publicly-stated opinion of me. I never heard her say something negative about me to someone else, including my dad, my brother, my husband and my extended family. Because of that, I cringe when I hear moms saying less-than-complimentary things about their child when the child is within hearing distance. Even a seemingly harmless sentence about something negative – "she is terrible at math" – can make a lasting impression on a child. She cautions moms that children hear every word spoken about them, even if it seems like they are preoccupied with play. And she would caution them that their children's opinion of themselves was being formed by what their mom says about them. Her go-to phrase to moms (and dads) – "If you can't say something good about your child, don't say anything at all."

Molly's Meatball Lesson #61

Talk to and about your children the way you'd like your children to talk to and about you.

Don't Be A Cop!

"In wrath remember mercy."

— HABAKKUK 3:2

Something happened to my mother when I became a mother. She became a grandmother. When I became a mother, my mom's relationship with me changed because now she was my son's grandmother. She had a new and shiny responsibility: to help me raise my son. My brother and his wife, Cece, had three children before I had one. So my son was her fourth grandchild, but the first time I knew her as a grandmother. To say Mom loves her grandchildren is as much as an understatement as to say the sun is hot. She loved, loved, and loved her grandchildren. When they were little, Mom did not live close to us geographically so she had to use the telephone and the postal service to "help" me raise my son. I loved and needed her advice. I came to rely on her wisdom on an almost daily basis. She offered it freely. It was not unusual for me to receive mail from her with a clipping from an article she had read. I remember the one about how too much licorice could cause headaches. This was because Philip had been eating licorice the last time we were with her and she thought he had eaten too much. If a situation required my immediate attention, Mom would call me. For example, one day when my son was eight years old there was a tragic event that took place in New York City. The media there was covering the story of an eight-year-old boy who fell to his death from the roof of a 40-story apartment building earlier that morning. His parents owned a small grocery store that operated on the street level of the apartment building. Their son would spend most of his days in the store with his parents. One day, one of the tenants of the building had locked herself out of her apartment. She asked the boy's parents if he could come and help her try to get in to her apartment. They agreed. What the boy's parents didn't know is that her plan was to tie a rope around the boy's waist, and lower him from the roof so that he could climb inside an open window and then unlock her door. The rope broke and the boy fell to his death. My mother was heartbroken for these parents, and wanted to be sure that this never happened to us.

She called, told me the story in tears, and said, "Please warn Philip that if anyone ever wants to tie a rope around his waist and lower him from an apartment building, he shouldn't do it." I knew Mom's heart was in a panic, but we were living in a very rural area of Pennsylvania. We were surrounded by hundreds of acres of farmland. There was not a 40-story building for hundreds of miles. I repeated her instructions back to her, "OK. Mom let me get this straight. If anyone every wants to tie a rope around Philip's waist and lower him from an apartment building, I should tell him he shouldn't do that?" She got my sarcasm. We both had a good laugh.

"The letter kills, but the Spirit gives life."

— 2 CORINTHIANS 3:6

However, some of her other grandmotherly, raising-kids advice was truly wisdom. Mom said to me, "Look, sometimes when you were younger and I saw you doing something you knew you shouldn't be doing, I didn't let you know that I had seen you do it. Because if you knew that I had seen you, then I needed to discipline you for doing it. I would be disciplining you all day long. What kind of good would that do? You will make your child a nervous wreck if all you do is discipline all the time. As a mother, you need to choose your battles. There are some things you cannot and should not ignore. But there are some things you should just look away from and let it go. I didn't want you to grow up thinking that your mother was like a cop, watching your every move, waiting to pounce on you for disobeying a small little guideline. Sometimes, mercy is what's needed instead of the law. Ask the Lord for the wisdom to know when you need mercy and when you need to enforce the letter of the law. And He will give you the wisdom to decide."

Molly's Meatball Lesson #62

Choose your parenting battles. Don't be a cop. If the crime is small, and your child doesn't know you've seen them break a small rule, then look away.
Let it go.

- **Be Happy.** When I think about my childhood, I remember laughter. I remember joy. I remember that my mom was always making light of things that might weigh me down. We were always laughing, smiling, happy and joyful. I remember "The Rice Story." Above our piano were some sketches with oriental background and people. The people were working in the rice fields. So she would sit on the piano bench with me at her side and tell me the continuing saga of The Rice People. She would tinkle one or two keys to provide her background music. It was not anything close to playing. It was Mom just making noise. The story progressed with the music corresponding to the situation being describes. I loved it. The story would be so fascinating to me. Then she would bang the keys down loudly, and I'd look up to hear her say, "Oops. They just fell down." We laughed and laughed. It was obvious she wanted to be with me. She wanted to be next to me. I remember how fun it was to hear these stories. She was happy. Happiness is always a choice. My mom always chose to be happy with me. And because of that I remember having a happy life. All my life. Sometimes her delivery itself was hilarious, even though the wisdom was pure gold. She'd say to some of her girls at church, "Some of you are such cranky mothers. Stop being such a crank all the time! You're making your kids sick. Cut it out!" There is always something to be happy about.

- **Be Thankful.** I'm not going to take up lots of room here about being thankful. This is a spiritual issue for every person. We must choose to focus on what we have rather than what we don't have. As I was growing up, several times a day, I heard both my parents say, out loud, "Thank You, Lord. Thank You, Lord". My dad could be fixing the washer and he would be saying, "Thank You, Lord." They said out loud, "Thank you, Lord" at least 50 times a day. I don't know what they were thanking Him for but I knew they were thankful. You may not realize how infectious a mom's attitude is. Mom would say, "Choose to be thankful in front of your child. There is always something to be thankful about."
- **Cast Your Burdens on Jesus, Not Your Kid.** I've heard Mom say to women: "Don't expect your children to carry your burdens for you. Your kid is not you psychiatrist." There's nothing wrong

with being transparent and honest with your children about things that are going on in your life. But Mom didn't think it was wise for a mom to expect her child to bear the burdens of life for her. For example, one single mom she knew hated her job. She felt she was being mistreated at work. In truth, this mom's life was going through a very difficult season. Her 11-year-old son confided to my mom and me after church one Sunday, telling us he couldn't sleep at night because he was so worried about how mean the people at work were being to his mom. This mom, alone and lonely, had elevated her kid into an adult emotionally. And he wasn't. I heard Mom commiserate with her about being alone and needing someone to talk to. She said, "Call me and talk to me. But this is a burden an 11-year-old should not have been expected to carry." The mom followed her advice, and soon they were close friends. And her son began sleeping like a baby.

Molly's Meatball Lesson #63

Keep your burdens to yourself - unless you are giving them to Jesus.
He has the strength to carry every burden. Your children do not.

As you might guess, Mom's advice and wisdom to me was not limited to being a wife and mother. In the next chapter, I'll share some "sound-bite" advice that I carried – and still carry through each day. You might like to adopt some of her advice for yourself. Or not.

9

YOU NEVER KNOW

Recipes For Everyday Living

"The words of King Lemuel. The sayings his mother taught him"

— PROVERBS 31:1

I love this guy Lemuel. He's a king and he's writing down his words and he makes sure he gives the credit for these sayings where it belongs: his mother. Proverbs 31 is written by a guy who loves his mother. Jewish tradition hints that King Lemuel might be another name for King Solomon, the son of David. If that's true (and we don't know this sure) then these sayings of his mother are the sayings of Bathsheba. She is famous for her adultery with King David. Wouldn't it be ironic if the much admired Proverbs 31 Woman were sayings by the former adulteress Bathsheba? (Note to all the Bible scholars out there: this is just conjecture. Writer's musings.) God used Bathsheba's life to influence her son – and through him, the world. This gives hope to all of us who have made mistakes in our past. God is never finished using our lives.

In this chapter I will follow King Lemuel's lead. A large percentage of my mother's recipes for living life were taught to me in the sayings she said. Every day of my life, one or more of my mother's sayings will pop in to my mind and give me some wisdom and guidance about something happening at that moment.

Here then are: *"The Words of Marie Armenia. The sayings her mother taught her."*

"You Never Know"

"For my thoughts are not your thoughts, neither are your ways my ways, declares the LORD. As the heavens are higher than the earth, so are my ways higher than your ways and my thoughts than your thoughts."

— ISAIAH 55:8-9

Of all the sayings my mother taught me, this one – "you never know" – has been the one I hear most often in the catacombs and recesses of my brain. For me these three words have been part aggravating and part "inspirating." I didn't want to live my life with never-ending never knowing. Mom doesn't say "you never know" as if to say, "Oh, well. Just accept not knowing." Oh, no! She says it as a challenge. She says it as a way of reminding me that I will never know unless I try. I will never get the answer to a question unless I ask. She taps in to my God-given over-the-top curiosity and inspires me to go for it. I don't want to "never know." I want to know.

For example this would be a typical "you never know" conversation with my mom. When I was in high school, I really wanted to be on the Student Council. I wanted to be student body treasurer. I was unsure of myself so I didn't register. When I got home from school on the last day registrations were allowed, I told my mom that the registration period had ended that day. I explained I had been unsure of my chances of winning. Mom didn't care if I was student body treasurer or not. To be unsure of myself was what bothered my mother the most. Mom said," You may win. You may lose. You never know. Why don't you call the teacher in charge of this at school and ask her if you can still register if I drive you to the school?"

I answered, "I don't think she's there."

"Well, you never know."

I continued, "And if she is, I don't think she'll answer the phone."

"You never know."

"And if she answers the phone, I don't think she will let me do that."

Mom said, "You never know."

Mom was right. I wanted to know, and if I didn't at least try, I would never know.

I was elected to Student Council by the biggest margin of victory in the school's history. Now I know.

A few years ago, the air conditioning on our SUV exploded two months after the warranty had expired. It was going to cost us lots of money to replace it. I explained the horrible timing to my mother. I whined, "It's not covered under the warranty anymore."

"It's so close in time. Ask them if they might fix it under the warranty."

"Mom. The warranty has expired. Auto dealerships don't go around honoring warranties two months after they have expired."

"You never know."

I took the challenge. I asked. They installed a new unit without charging us a cent. Now I know.

One of the most precious things I own is something I got for free. My mom and I were shopping together one day and I stopped at a department store in the mall. I bought myself some new makeup and some skincare products. I spent more money than I wanted to because my mother kept urging me as I looked at each item, "Get it. Get it." As it turns out, Mom paid for everything I bought. Speaking of, it just occurred to me that I have not mentioned before how generous my mother is. I never did without one thing because the moment she saw I wanted something, she made it her duty to see that I had it. In every room of my home there is something my mother bought for me. Furniture or an appliance I needed. Half the clothes in my closet are things my mom has gifted to me. She has been very, very generous to me and to all the members of her family. She is a giver with a capital G.

Anyway, she bought me the makeup and skincare cream. And as the salesperson was ringing us up, I noticed a really pretty rust-colored leather make-up kit. The sign next to it said it came free with a purchase of perfume. I didn't use that perfume. The smallest size cost $80. My mom saw me looking at it. "Do you want that?", she asked. I explained it only came with the purchase of the perfume. "Ask her if you might have one. You never know." I wouldn't do it. So she did. The woman gave me the make-up kit.. Now I know. Every time I use it, it speaks to me about asking for something because as mom says, "You never know what someone will say unless you ask. They might say yes and you will have what you asked for. Or they might say no. You won't die if they say no. At least you asked."

I cherish that make-up case. Now I know.

It isn't just high school elections, auto air-conditioning units and make-up cases that her words inspired in me. Throughout my life, the words' You never know" have been " the catalyst to try something, ask for something or be something I didn't think I could be.

These three words have most affected my history and my future when she is talking to me about the Lord and His ways. She reminds me that no one can ever know what God intends to do in a situation. At pivotal junctures in my life, Mom has asked me questions. "Did Moses know God was going to split the Red Sea? Did David expect to grow up and become the King of Israel? Did the woman caught in the act of adultery know that Jesus was going to forgive her? Did Mary and Martha know Jesus was going to raise their brother from the dead?" Then Mom would say, "No Marie, they didn't know. Because you never know exactly what God is going to do. But He does. That's why our faith must be in Him and His character and His Word and His promises."

I think most of us would like to know before we have to step out. But that isn't faith. Throughout the ears, Mom has instilled faith in my heart when she has said, "You never know which prayer requests God will grant. So ask Him for everything all the time. You never know which opportunity He places before you is a door He is opening for your gifts and ministry. Mom reminds me over and over that God's ways are not our ways, and you never know when He wants to split a sea in your life or resurrect something that has died. You never know what it feels like to have your guilty conscience healed unless you ask. You never know what God will say unless you ask Him to speak to your heart.

You never know unless you ask. And then you know.

Molly's Meatball Lesson #64

As long as you accept that you never know it all, then you will always
be willing to inquire of The One who does.

"Dupamend Solo A La Dupamend – You Never Know, Part 2"

"He who searches our hearts knows the mind of the Spirit, because the
Spirit intercedes for God's people in accordance with the will of God."

— ROMANS 8:27

Mom always says this particular saying to me in Italian, and it sounds something like what I wrote in the title. It translates: "Only the spoon that stirs the soup knows all the ingredients in the soup." It's like Part 2 of "You Never Know." Mom isn't talking soup; she's talking people. She says it as a reminder to me that "you never know what someone is going through." The spoon that's in the pot – absorbing everything, enduring the heat, living in the middle of it all, mixing the soup – is the real expert on what the soup is all about. Only the person intimately involved and immersed in the situation truly knows what's going on. The rest of us are mere observers with opinions, but not necessarily the truth. With this saying Mom is exhorting me to never assume someone's life is as perfect as they portray it or as bad as it seems. You never know why someone acts the way they do or reacts the way they do. You never know what's really going on. You never know what burdens someone's heart is bearing. You never know the whole story. Even if you think you do. When it comes to people, Mom always taught me that I am called to pray for them. I am not called to criticize, condemn, look down on, or feel superior or inferior to any other human being on earth. I am called to pray for friends, family and my enemies. Pray. Pray. Pray. And although I never know what someone is going through, the Holy Spirit does. So I can simply ask the Holy Spirit how to pray for other people. And when I ask, He will answer. Suddenly I feel like the spoon in that pot. God gives me compassion that I didn't have before I started to pray. Somehow I know that person is carrying a burden that weighs them down, even though I may not have specifics. At times I will begin to sense that there has been deep wounds and great abuse. It's amazing what the Holy Spirit does when you pray for someone else. Mom says, " There are so many things you never know. But, you always know that praying for someone is the right thing to do."

Molly's Meatball Lesson #65

Don't assume you know the whole story of someone else's life.
You never know. But God does. Pray.

Getting Off That Subject Now

"Finally, brothers and sisters, whatever is true, whatever is noble,
whatever is
right, whatever is pure, whatever is lovely, whatever is admirable—if
anything is excellent or praiseworthy—think about such things."

— PHILIPPIANS 4:8

Not only does Mom have self-control over her own speech, but she controls her family's conversation whenever she was around. When a conversation has the potential to create hurt feelings, Mom simply says, "Getting off that subject now..." and turn the conversation in a completely different direction. If we try to go back to the subject she has just told us to get off of, she simply repeats, "Getting off that subject. Now!" When I was growing up, if a conversation veered toward gossip about someone or something inappropriate, Mom would say those words, "Getting off that subject now." If we were with a group of people or a public meeting, and one of us happened to bring up something she felt was private or unbecoming to be talking about, she would smile and calmly say, "Getting off that subject now." Those five words were all we needed to hear. We got off that subject. And we got off it now.

Molly's Meatball Lesson #66

Just because you feel like talking about something doesn't mean you should.
When staying on a subject is causing division or sin, get off that subject.

It's The Appearance of Evil

"I have the right to do anything," you say—but not everything is beneficial. "I have the right to do anything"—but not everything is constructive."

— 1 Corinthians 10:23

"Abstain from all appearance of evil."

— 1 Thessalonians 5:22 (KJV)

Mom doesn't try to look perfect, as you may have already figured out, but she certainly isn't going to do anything that could appear to look wrong or sinful. She isn't going to give anyone any cause to doubt that Jesus is real and pure and alive in her life. I cannot count the times she had asked me to consider laying down my right to do something. It wasn't so that I could look holy but so that no one could think that something we were doing appeared evil or sinful.

For example, after Phil and I graduated from high school and he had a car, we had a lot more freedom and time by ourselves. My parents were often out or at church or visiting people. They always parked their car on the street in front of our house so it was obvious they weren't home. This meant that Phil would often come to pick me up for a date when my parents were away. One day my mom said, "Look, you and Phil are at the age where if you want to cross the line and sin with your bodies, there is plenty of opportunity for you to do that. I pray that you will obey God and stay pure until your wedding night. (We did.) That's between the two of you and God. I cannot be with you all the time. The neighbors know that Daddy and I are often not home when Phil comes to get you. Even if you don't do one thing wrong – and I trust the two of you – I am asking that when he comes to pick you up, please let him stay in the car until you are ready."

I obeyed her and I didn't think much of it until the three days before our wedding. The woman who lived across the street came over to give us a wedding gift. She told my mom, "A few of the neighbors have been so surprised and impressed watching your daughter's boyfriend and your daughter as they have dated. We noticed he never came in the house when you and your husband weren't home." Who knew the neighbors were watching us? Mom did. Our neighbor said she saw something "pure" in the way our family lived our life. My mom brought the conversation around to the Lord and how it is only Jesus who is pure. That woman, who had resisted my mom's sharing the gospel for decades, gave her life to the Lord a few weeks later.

Mom's policy about this wasn't a legalistic attempt to look like we were sinless. It was simply a reminder to take a step back and look at my actions and be sure that I was willing to lay something down if it might cause someone else to stumble. She says, "God knows what you are and aren't doing. That's between you and God. But people only know what they see." If it looks sinful, don't do it.

Molly's Meatball Lesson #67

Having the right to do something doesn't mean you should do it.
Your actions must always be the actions of Jesus.

"Don't Bring Attention To Your Flaws"

"How beautiful you are, my darling! Oh, how beautiful!"

— SONG OF SONGS 1:15

Because of the transparent way Mom lived her life, I grew up not being afraid to be myself. I'd rather have one friend who loves the real me than a hundred friends I have to be false with. But every now and then she would hear me speaking about something about myself that I didn't like, or mentioning to someone that I was not good at something. She didn't like this at all. "Don't bring attention to your flaws, Marie. No one notices what seems like a big deal to you. When you point it out, then they notice it." I try not to.

Mostly, the attitude behind this saying of hers helped me in my relationship with God. So often, it feels good in our flesh to look at our flesh. To see what's wrong with us and to continue to act like God is keeping score. We are tempted to pray pitiful prayers pointing out the weaknesses that Jesus came to die for. Mom's basis for her opinion of God's opinion of her came straight from God's Word. She believes she is whatever God says she is. When I was growing up, Mom didn't pray prayers that pointed out her flaws to God. Sure, she confessed her sin and knew the Lord would cleanse her from all unrighteousness as soon as she did (1 John 1:9). I never heard her say, "Oh God, I'm so weak. I'm such a failure. I'm not what I should be. I'm not who I should be." She didn't pray prayers of how weak she was; she reminded God she knew how powerful He is. She didn't pray prayers about her sinfulness; she thanked God for giving her righteousness. Her attitude about her standing with God has always been a reflection of these verses in Psalm 103: *"The LORD is compassionate and gracious, slow to anger, abounding in love. He will not always accuse, nor will he harbor his anger forever; he does not treat us as our sins deserve or repay us according to our iniquities For as high as the heavens are above the earth, so great is his love for those who fear him; as far as the east is from the west, so far has he removed our transgressions from us. As a father has compassion on his children, so the* Lord *has compassion on those who fear him; for he knows how we are formed, he remembers that we are dust"* (vv. 8-14).

To Mom there is a great distinction between prayers confessing sin to God and being forgiven for it because of the blood of Jesus and praying prayers that remind God how flawed you are. As if He doesn't know. He sees your heart better than the best MRI. He knows your thoughts. He knows your motives. There's nothing about yourself that you can tell Him that He doesn't already know. The beauty of Jesus makes you beautiful to God. You aren't flawed to Him. You are beautiful. *"God made him who had no sin to be sin for us, so that in him we might become the righteousness of God"* (2 Cor. 5:21). Stop pointing out your flaws and focus on the beauty that is Jesus.

Molly's Meatball Lesson #68

Don't waste time pointing out your flaws to God.
Instead thank Him for Jesus. In Him you are completely beautiful
and righteous.

"He Was Reviled"

"He was reviled, reviled not again; when he suffered, he threatened not;
but committed himself to him that judgeth righteously."

— 1 Peter 2:23, KJV

I wrote about this verse in a previous chapter, but I didn't mention there that this was one of her oft-used sayings. I have always been a feisty little fighter of a person. Defending myself, explaining myself, wanting justice for every wrong. I'm a tough girl. And yet my mother always cautioned me about defending myself, retaliating and wanting revenge. When I complain to her about someone who was being unfair – as a child and even now as an adult – she says, *"He was reviled and He reviled not again."* Another Bible translation puts it this way, *"When they hurled their insults at him, he did not retaliate"* (NIV). Yes, Mom. One day I thought of a defense to this unreasonable expectation of hers that I should not revile. I said, "Mom, I'm not like Jesus. OK?" To which she replied, "But you should be, Marie. You should be."

Molly's Meatball Lesson #69

A Christian who doesn't understand that God's plan is to make her look and
act like Jesus is a Christian who will never comprehend why God is allowing what God is allowing.

"Tell Him To Tell Me"

"Do not be quick with your mouth, do not be hasty in your heart to utter anything before God."

— ECCLESIASTES 5:2

Recently, I had a friend call me in despair. A woman in her church had come up to her with "a word from the Lord" about her family's decision to move to another state. This woman claims the Lord told her to "correct" them about things they had done while living in their present location. There was nothing redemptive, encouraging or kind about her words. There was nothing close to love. It seemed as if the woman was envious of their financial status and many other things. I told my friend what my grandmother used to say to people who came to her saying things like this. Nonnon passed it on to her daughters, and my mother passed it on to me. Mom has always been open to correction or exhorting from a fellow believer. She knows that God knows she wants to hear His voice. Wouldn't God speak directly to a person who is longing to hear His voice? Diligently seeking Him? Of course He will. So Mom would simply tell whomever came to her, "God knows me and how much I long to hear His voice. I'm not refusing to accept what you just told me. I'm just asking you to ask God to tell me what you think He told you to tell me." And that was that. Sometimes He did. Sometimes He didn't.

Molly's Meatball Lesson #70

Just because someone says God told her to tell you something doesn't mean that God told her to tell you something.

These are just a few of the sayings of Molly Bruno. She has many more but it's time to move on to the next amazing thing about my mom. Her dreams and visions.

10

IF YOU EVER SEE A BIG BLACK BULL IN FRONT OF YOUR CAR!

Recipe For The Dreams God Gives

"For God does speak—now one way, now another— though
no one perceives it.
In a dream, in a vision of the night, when deep sleep falls on people,
as they slumber in their beds."

— JOB 33:14-15

I could not write a book about my mother if I didn't include an aspect of her life that is something that doesn't happen to most people I know, including me. God literally speaks to her in dreams and visions. Yes, yes, yes. I know that some of you reading this don't believe He does that anymore. That's OK; you can skip this chapter. But you would be missing out on some really amazing stuff if you did. So then let me set the stage for you. Mom doesn't seek out visions, she doesn't ask for dreams. They come. She prays about whatever she has dreamt and moves on. She doesn't interpret dreams and visions. She doesn't get into anything that even suggests she lives her life – or instructs others to live their lives - by her dreams and visions. Mom lives her life by God's Word. She's not some weirdo, dream dreamer. OK. I have qualified enough. For as long as I can remember, my mother had dreams that had a direct connection to something going on in her life or the lives of others. Her dreams always created a desire to pray for and about whatever and whoever was in the dream. The following instances are true. And as with all the unbelievable things about my unbelievable mother, I have witnesses.

The Black Bull Story

We talk on the phone first thing in the morning. Usually she will share something she read in the Bible that morning, or she will share something she heard on Christian TV during the night, and sometimes she will share a dream she had. Her retelling is always passionate and animated. She relates the dream as if it really happened. I say to her, "Mom, this was a dream, not a report on cable news." She doesn't mind my irreverence. One particular day she said, "Oh, Marie I couldn't wait for you to call this morning. Listen to this dream I had about you. I dreamed that you were driving in your white car (an SUV) and a huge black bull charged at you. He had you pinned against the front of your car and you were screaming, 'Help!' In the dream, I couldn't get to you fast enough, and you finally just fell to the street, limp and bleeding."

"Gee, Mom, I'm so glad I called. What a great way to start my day. How great to hear your dream about me being gored to death by a bull against the front of my white car. Wonderful. Great. Thanks. What did you eat before you went to sleep last night?'

"Marie, don't make fun. The dream was real."

"OK, Mom. Then pray that if I ever see a big black bull, God will protect me from getting gored to death on the front of my car."

"Marie! Don't make fun of my dream. That's exactly what I will pray."

"OK. Mom. Getting off that subject now..."

And we talked about other things.

When I was finished speaking to my mother, my husband asked, "What was that about a bull?" I retold my mother's dream to him. We shook our heads like we didn't believe she couldn't see how ridiculous this dream was. A big black bull? Really, Mom?

Five weeks later, I am pulling in to my neighborhood and there are police cars and fire trucks all over the place. I stopped to ask one of the police officers what was going on. He explained, "The farm next door had a breech in their fence and all the cattle are wandering through your subdivision. We're helping the farmer and his crew by keeping the cars from hitting any of the animals." As I turned the corner, at the end of a cul-de-sac, I saw a huge black cow with great big horns on his head. It was majestic animal. I wanted a picture. (Note to reader: This city girl didn't know that most cows don't have huge horns.) So I stopped my white SUV just a few feet in front of the big black cow with horns and decided to take a picture. As this city girl stood there taking the picture, the big black cow with horns started charging for her. What? What a cranky cow. I jumped in my car and pulled away as the big black cow with horns was mere inches from my car.

When I got home, I mentioned this to Phil, who said, "That wasn't a cow; that was a bull." An hour later, a full hour later, my brain exploded with the realization that this was my mother's dream coming true. That maybe because she had the dream and prayed for God to protect me from a big black bull, He did! She prayed as I mocked her. I called her to tell her what had just happened. I told her I was sorry for not believing the dream might have been God warning her to pray. She said, "I forgive you. Next time believe me!" Yes, Mom.

The Black Car Story

The unusual thing is not that she had the dream but that I didn't take it seriously. I had been a witness to this kind of stuff happening all my life. The one that stands out the most happened when I was about 12 years old. My cousins and were at "The Lake - house my mother purchased with her sisters when we were all babies. She was not there on this particular week because there was something going on at church at home in Staten Island. The lake was nestled close to the Tri-State area, where New York, New Jersey and Pennsylvania come together. Decades ago, when we were all children, it was a very remote area, not very populated, and surrounded by mountains. One day, my cousin Patricia and I decided to walk to the other side of the lake just to have something to do. It was about three miles around. We walked the full circle of the lake and when we came out the other side, it required that we walk about a mile on the shoulder of the road along the main highway to get back to the side of the lake where we lived. Even though this was the biggest highway anywhere near the lake, it was still a pretty remote location. As we walked along the shoulder, a car pulled up behind us, driving slowly behind us as we walked. A man was driving the car with his window open, and he called out to us, "Girls, come here. I need directions." Immediately, even at my young age, I knew we should not go near the car.

"No, we can't come," I said firmly and Patricia and I started walking faster. The man drove to keep us with us. As he drove, he was saying some very obscene and scary things to us. We were terrified. I knew we couldn't outrun his car.

We kept walking faster and faster. He said to us, "I am just going to run my car into the both of you so that you both fall off the side of this highway and in to the valley below. No one will ever find you." And with that, he backed up his car and started to come toward us.

Just then a car was driving by and I jumped into the highway and screamed for them to stop. They drove right by us. And then for some reason, this evil man made a U-turn and drove off in the opposite direction. Patricia and I were hysterical and terrified. We ran the entire way back to the safety of our house and our aunts and cousins.

As we were running in the front door, and before we could say a word, we saw my Aunt Ruthie, Patricia's mom, picking up the telephone that was ringing. On the phone was my mother calling from New York. She was in a panic, "Do you know where Marie and Patricia are?"

Aunt Ruthie answered, "Yes, they are both just walked in the door. Why?"

Mom said, "I was laying on the sofa about to take a nap and suddenly I saw a black car with a man in it. He was going to do something horrible to Marie and Patricia. It was a vivid real dream, as real as if I was seeing it with my own eyes. I saw the license plate on the car. I prayed immediately that God would deliver them from this evil person. But if they are there, I don't know what this dream was about."

Aunt Ruthie, unaware of what had just happened said, "No, Molly. They're fine." And then she turned to us and said, "Your mother just saw a man in a black car trying to harm the two of you."

We fell to our knees in shock. When we told everyone what had just happened, it was just one more reminder that God is real and speaks to those of us who are willing to listen. I believe the reason the man suddenly made a U-turn and drove off in the opposite direction is because God awakened my mother and showed her what was going on. I am thankful He knew she would pray a prayer filled with authority and power. As we spoke to the State Police about the incident, we offered to give them the guy's license plate number. We explained my mom had seen it in a dream. They respectfully declined.

She's Going To Have A Baby

Infertility is a heartbreaking thing for any couple to have to endure. For years, our friends Bob and Dene Williams tried unsuccessfully to conceive. The fertility treatments did not work, and the longer they tried, the more discouraged they became. My mom visited us in Tennessee and happened to meet Dene. Dene, knowing my mother's prayer reputation, asked her to pray that she might have a child. I still remember my mom placing her hand on Dene's abdomen and praying Dene's request. About a year later, on a Friday night, Mom called and said, "Marie, I was praying and the Lord brought your friend Dene to my mind. Please tell her that I feel strongly that God is going to answer her request and she is going to be pregnant soon." I listened to Mom and then got busy and forgot to tell Dene.

Saturday morning, Mom asked if I had called Dene. I had not. "Please tell her that the Lord has impressed me strongly that He is going to allow her to be pregnant. Very, very soon." So now, to be honest, since God didn't speak to me, and since I didn't want to look foolish, I conveniently "forgot" to tell Dene what my mother felt strongly. Sunday afternoon after church, Molly decided to take matters into her own hands when I told her I still hadn't given her message to Dene. "Give me her phone number and I will call her myself," she insisted. I said, "No, I will call her, Mom."

That afternoon I called Dene. I told her what Mom said. She said, "You know at any other time in the past few years I would have welcomed your call and your mother's feelings. But this Friday we are on our way to pick up our adopted son and I do not really want to have two babies at the same time. So, thanks, but I don't really receive what you are saying."

Three weeks later, the home pregnancy test confirmed what my mother had been saying all along. Dene's pregnancy was confirmed two weeks after picking up her newly adopted son Jude. I told my mom. She wasn't surprised. Less than a year later, Isabella (Bella) arrived.

"7-0-2-2"

One Monday morning, I called Mom and like so many times before she had a dream the night before. She said, "Marie, you have to help me pray for a woman I dreamed about. In the dream, my phone rang and I picked it up and the woman on the other end was crying hysterically. She was so afraid of something. And I kept telling her that only God was able to help her. Only God could take her fear. In the dream, I kept telling her that God was close, that God was near. I was so concerned for her and I cannot get the dream off my mind. The dream was so real, that I even noticed part of the number on my caller ID in the dream. The last four digits were 7-0-2-2. Do we know anyone whose phone number ends in 7-0-2-2?" I couldn't think of anyone we knew, friends or family, who had that number. I checked all my contacts. Nothing. No one. Mom fervently prayed for this woman, whoever she was. I gently reminded her that it was only a dream, and maybe there wasn't an actual woman anywhere whose phone number ended in 7-0-2-2 who needed prayer. She ignored me and kept praying for her, "Lord, comfort her. Lord, be near her. Lord, help her." It was her constant prayer, all day and every time she woke up at night.

On the following Thursday Phil and I took my parents out for the day. We left in the morning and got home about 4 pm. My parent's phone does not have an answering machine. If you call her and she's not home, you cannot leave a message. But she has gotten into the habit of checking her caller ID to see who has called while she's out. When we got home that afternoon, lo and behold, someone had called her from New York and the last four digits of the phone number were 7-0-2-2. What?

Mom picked up the phone and called the number. When the person on the other end picked up she said, "This is Molly Bruno. Did you call me?" As it turns out, the caller was a distant cousin whose doctor had told her earlier that day that he suspected she had cancer. She was beyond distressed. I could hear her crying even though I wasn't on the phone. My mom told her about the dream she had and that she had been praying for her since Monday. "Look how much God loves you," she said. "He had someone praying for you before you even knew you needed prayer." This brought comfort to the woman. The next day she called my mother to tell her that the test results were negative. She did not have cancer. And thus began my mother's journey to explain the love of God to a distant cousin – and to ask her if she knew for sure where she would go on the day she does die.

Marie, Take Me To Where the Prostitutes Hang Out!

It's not every day your 91-year-old mother asks you to drive her to the place where the prostitutes work. "I don't know where that section might be, Mom," I answered, "And why do you want to go there?" At my age, I know better than to be surprised at anything my mother says. One of her prayer practices is that whenever she happens to wake up in the middle of the night, she asks the Lord who might need prayer. She is usually 100 percent accurate about hearing the Lord's voice about praying for someone. Invariably, she will call them and tell them, "The Lord called me to pray for you. Is everything all right?" That person always responds that they needed prayer. It's just a testimony to the power of the Holy Spirit to show us who needs prayer and when. But on this particular morning when we spoke, Mom was very emotional and crying.

She said, "Last night, when I asked the Lord who to pray for, suddenly I saw a woman's face. Marie, it was as clear as if she were standing in front of me. She has a round face, dark hair, and she was crying. Sobbing. And she is a prostitute. And she was crying, and saying, 'I am so tired of this. Is there any hope for me? Is there any way out of this life?' And she is desperate, and thinking of ending her life because of her desperation. And I was talking to her and telling her, 'I am praying for you. God sees you. He will help you.' I want to meet her. And I want to tell her that God hear her prayer and that I am praying for her."

Mom asked me to post the story on my Facebook page and ask people to pray for the prostitute. She has asked the Lord to let her meet this woman. I am in the process of trying to bring her to some ministries and agencies in Nashville who minister to women trapped in a life of prostitution. She also asked me to ask you to ask the Lord to lead her to the woman she saw. Will you?

These kinds of things in Mom's life are numerous and lovely. She tells of the moment, when she was a little girl and was sick. She looked out the window and saw an angel. The angel spoke to her in Italian and told her she would be fine. She tells of hearing a loud voice when she was a small child. Everything out of the ordinary that has happened in her life has been a catalyst for prayer. Every story. More prayers.

Molly's Meatball Lesson #71

*Don't expect God to speak to you in dreams and visions,
but don't expect Him not to.*

11

RESURRECTION GROUND

The Recipe For Living Forever

*"We wait for the blessed hope—the appearing of the glory of our great God
and Savior, Jesus Christ, who gave himself for us to redeem us from
all wickedness and to purify for himself a people that are his very own,
eager to do what is good." in their beds."*

— Titus 2:13-14

Truth is, I expected to be writing this final chapter differently than I am being forced to write it. A few months ago, we happened to be driving past the cemetery where my mother and my father have pre-purchased burial plots. She got out and stood on the plots and with joy in her voice and holy reverence in her eyes, she announced to my father, "Honey! Look! This is our Resurrection Ground! This is where Jesus is going to resurrect our earthly bodies!" I expected to write about that cute and hopeful incident and end this book about Mom with a chapter that talked about her future hope is to be with the Lord. You know, like in the future. Like 100 years from now.

I never expected to be writing about how, on April 1, 2015, after weeks of trying to figure out why Mom was feeling so extremely weak and after a night of her experiencing intense pain on her upper right side, the doctors at Vanderbilt University Hospital informed us that her weakness and pain was coming from gallbladder cancer. Advanced. Stage Four. Nothing they could do. "Just a matter of days, maybe a few weeks" they spoke to me in whispers.

What? You've got to be kidding me. Days? Weeks? What? She's stronger than any of us. Just a few weeks ago, she was doing all her work around her house, all her laundry, and cleaning and cooking and taking care of Dad. She's invincible. On the way to the hospital that morning, she got me to promise her that I would just tell her the truth about whatever the doctors said. I promised. She doesn't have the greatest hearing and so I repeated to her what the doctor just said. It was surreal to hear myself saying to my beautiful, beautiful Mom, "Mom, the doctor says you have cancer in your gallbladder. He says you don't have long to live. He says it could be just days, and at the most, just weeks." I looked into those beautiful eyes of hers as she sat on the hospital bed listening and her eyes looked directly in to mine and she said, "I am not moved by these words. The Lord is in control. The Lord will take me when the Lord has ordained to take me. Today. Tomorrow. Next week. I'm ready."

When I started this book I planned that the last chapter would cover her future since most of the book has covered her life. I envisioned speaking in theory about the hope she had that her death would be the beginning of eternal life. As I absorbed the words the doctor was saying, I was surprised that my mind jumped back to that happy scene of her dancing on her resurrection ground. It hit me that her resurrection ground might not be staying empty for as long as I assumed it would.

My mother, 92, is dying. As I type the words, I know it in my brain, but today, three weeks later, I still have her. She is weaker in body but still strong in her spirit. The kind doctors said to me, "Go home and make her comfortable." And that's exactly what I am doing. I promised her I would not leave her side no matter how long this season lasts. On that day in the hospital, she told the surgeons that her hope was in the Lord. She told them she was looking forward to seeing Jesus. She told them that she wasn't afraid to die. And she was telling the truth. As each team of doctors came in to discuss a different aspect of her diagnosis, she stopped them before they left her bedside and said, "Let's pray." Each doctor stopped and bowed their heads as she prayed for them. She asked the Lord to give them wisdom and understanding and compassion for their patients. She thanked the Lord for the way they had cared for her, praying loudly, "And finally, if any of these doctors don't know Jesus and have not given their lives to Him, please, Lord Jesus, reveal Yourself to every doctor standing here today. Don't let them die without You, Lord." And when she was finished praying, they would reverently slip out of her room. They asked her to stay overnight so they could monitor her and set her up with palliative care the next day. I stayed with her overnight. The next afternoon, as we were checking out of her hospital room to go home, one of the surgeons who'd been with us the day before came into the room. He was out of breath and said, "Oh, I'm so happy I got to see you before you leave. I wanted to say goodbye." He had taken the time to look her up and find out where her room was. He shared that as the team of doctors had their morning meeting, each doctor independently commented about the elderly woman who was filled with such hope as she heard such a hopeless diagnosis. He said, "You have profoundly touched every one of us who were privileged to interact with you. Even though it was for such a short time." She smiled and turned the focus back on him.

"Son", she asked the surgeon, "Do you know Jesus?"

"Well, I'm Baptist."

"Son, I didn't ask if you were Baptist. I asked if you know Jesus. Do you love Him? Do you know Him?"

"I do."

"That's good, son. That's good."

Molly's Meatball Lesson #72

Just because someone just told you that you're dying is no reason to forget they are dying too. Make sure they know Jesus.

Explanation Expectations

"Though he slay me, yet will I hope in him."

— Job 13:15

This being sick thing is a new experience for her. She has never been sick, hardly ever had a cold, never the flu or anything lingering. I wondered what prayer she might be praying during this season of illness that is leading to her death. So I asked her, "Mom, what are you praying about this situation?" She answered immediately, "What I always pray: that God's will be done. Whatever it is. I believe He can heal me and I am ready to see Him if He doesn't. It's all up to Him." And that's it. She does not have explanation expectations of her Heavenly Father. She said, "I'm 92 years old and God has blessed me all my life. If He has decided this is when He wants me to come home, then this is when I am going home." God has healed her many, many times. God has healed people she has prayed for many, many times. But God doesn't have to explain what He's doing and why He's doing it to Molly Bruno. Her accepting attitude of God and His will is the epitome of peace.

I, however, am having a difficult time accepting that I am going to soon be saying goodbye to my mother. I do not want to walk through life without her. And then I remember that Jesus understands. I pour this broken heart out to Him. In the Garden of Gethsemane, when the enormity of bearing the sin of all humanity was at hand, Jesus *"fell with his face to the ground and prayed, "My Father, if it is possible, may this cup be taken from me"* (Matt. 26:39). I **love** that God allowed this to be included in His Word. It encourages those of us who are facing terrible things and are in the middle of feeling like we are not able to bear what seems to be God's will for us. If anyone understands not wanting to drink the cup of suffering we see before us, it is Jesus. It encourages me that Jesus asked God for a way around the suffering and death. I am asking Him for a way around my mother's suffering and death. I would like for it to not happen, thank You very much. Jesus understands. Jesus understands. Jesus understands.

I want my mother to live at least 25 more years. Molly Bruno has so much life and love and power in her that if any person on earth could be effective for the Lord for another 25 years, it's her. So, here it is, now four weeks after her diagnosis, and if I were to write the truth, it's that I want my mother to be healed and whole. I don't care that she's 92. I want her to live to 192. I want my mother. I want my mother. He understands. He also understands that I want God's will more. Jesus wanted the cup to pass from Him. And I think the most important sentence in the history of humanity is the one Jesus spoke in the Garden of Gethsemane, *"Yet not as I will, but as you will"* (Matt. 26:39). It's the most important sentence anyone can ever speak, no matter the circumstance. I speak it today to my heavenly Father. And so does my mom. We yield to our Lord. No explanation expectation expected.

Molly's Meatball Lesson #73

The Kingdom of God is not a democracy. God is not required to explain.

Hope Trumps Grief

Brothers and sisters, we do not want you to be uninformed about those who sleep in death, so that you do not grieve like the rest of mankind, who have no hope. For we believe that Jesus died and rose again, and so we believe that God will bring with Jesus those who have fallen asleep in him."

— 1 THESSALONIANS 4:13-14

One of the blessings of this long goodbye is that I am here all day every day, and even some nights. In a strange way, it feels like my childhood again. Being with Mommy and Daddy in their house. It feels familiar. It feels safe. And I am reminded that's what God is doing in my mom's life. He's bringing her back home. Bringing her back to her "Daddy."

She will feel safe. It will feel familiar. She will feel secure. In the meantime, death sentence or not, she continues to focus on encouraging others. When her phone rings (and it rings constantly) with someone asking for prayer, she just prays a power-filled prayer. The fact that she is sicker than most of the people she is praying for doesn't matter to her. She always, always, always (did I say, always?) puts the needs of others first. Yesterday, I heard her pray for nine people who had called her. Nine people. I never once heard her say, "Hey, you should be praying for me." Nope. She just prayed the Word of God, in faith, and then took a short nap. She cried with a mother whose son is leaving home, she prayed with a friend who just got home from the hospital, she offered hope to a wife whose husband just lost his job, and a family member leaving on a trip. She reminded them that God is faithful. God keeps His promises. In all these weeks, I have never seen her have a discouraged moment. I mean, seriously, who faces death this way? My mom, that's who.

Molly's Meatball Lesson #74

The best way to keep from being discouraged is to keep encouraging others.

Thank Him. The End.

"Rejoice always, pray continually, give thanks in all circumstances; for this is God's will for you in Christ Jesus."

— 1 THESSALONIANS 5:16-18

Her conversation is mostly Scripture. As she experiences some pain, she simply reminds herself that she should give thanks in everything. I hear her whispering it to herself as she falls asleep. The Word of God is so much part of her spirit that it seems like nothing but the Word of God flows out of her. She is simply reminding herself of God's promises to her. This unmovable, unshakeable woman whose faith in the goodness and promises of God is being tested now is not failing the test.

The people who come to care for her are the people she continues to pray for. Her Hospice nurse says her disease's progression is slower than expected and "atypical." As if Molly Bruno would do anything typically. I am seeing hope and thankfulness flow out of her. As she waits to die, she continues to praise. Rather than counting her days, she is counting her blessings. I am seeing the power of God in an ever shrinking and hardly eating 5'2" dynamo. She thanks God for every single thing. She thanks God for the piece of watermelon she just ate; for being able to lie on her side without pain. She thanks Him for the day she is having and for the peaceful night she had. Every morning when I walk into her bedroom, she smiles at me and says, "God gave us another day together." She thanks me for being a good daughter and she thanks God for giving me to her. "Lord, I asked you for this daughter and You gave her to me. Thank You. Thank You." She thanks the Lord for a family who loves her. She simply never stops thanking Him.

I'll be honest, though. Every now and then a flicker of panic flashes through my heart. It says, "How will I live without her? What will I do without her? How will I say goodbye?" But once again, she teaches me: choose to be thankful. I have made the choice to utter words of thankfulness to God during this season I had hoped would be far in our future. I am thanking God for giving me this time to say goodbye to this incredible woman who is my mother. I thank Him for all these mornings of drinking coffee together and listening to her tell me stories of her childhood, of her life, and how she loves me. (Oh, how my mother loves me.) I am thankful for a childhood filled with God. I am thankful that because of her, I gave my life to Jesus when I was eight years old. I am thankful that because of her, we will be together forever. I remember the day I was baptized. I am thankful that when she passes, she has left me the knowledge that she is with God, her Father. I don't have to wonder if she is at peace. I know it. I am thankful for all the miracles and answers to prayer I got to witness close up. I am thankful for her incredible humor. I am thankful for the tears-running-down-my-face-breath-robbing laughter that filled our lives together. I am thankful that, today, I get to hold her hand another day, hear her laugh another time, and look into those beautiful, beautiful green eyes one more day. I am thankful that I get the honor of caring for her, comforting her, and giving back to her just one tiny speck of all she has given to me. I am thankful that, as I type this, I can type that Molly Bruno is my mother and I don't yet have to say that Molly Bruno was my mother. Today is the only day that matters.

She cannot walk as steadily as she used to. As I walk behind her, with my arms under her arms to make sure she doesn't fall, I kiss her shoulders, her neck and her hair. I just kissed her face again. She smiled and kissed me back. And reminded me once again, "I prayed for you. I prayed for a daughter and God gave me the best of the best." After six decades of having me, she is still as thankful for me as the day I as born! Thank You, Lord. Thank You for letting me have my mom another day.

Molly's Meatball Lesson #75

Being thankful is always possible. Praise will bring peace.
Even in the most difficult seasons of life
there is always something to be thankful for.

The Place Of Prayer

During the filming of their latest movie, *War Room*, my mom and the Kendrick Brothers (*Fireproof, Courageous*) met and became friends. She became a prayer partner for *War Room* because my friend, Brenda Harris, who works for them told them that the character they were developing of an older, mentoring prayer warrior woman named Miss Clara reminded her of my mom. Stephen, Alex, and Shannon Kendrick told Brenda they would like to meet her. We set up a Skype session at my house. It was scheduled for 30 minutes but spanned almost three hours. Mom had never seen any of their movies and didn't have a clue who the Kendrick Brothers were but she really connected with Stephen. She saw something in him as he spoke. She commented after the first session,

"That boy really loves the Lord. His heart is sincere. I will definitely devote myself to praying for his movie."

And devote herself she did. She stayed up nights praying when they were filming a scene at night. She would forward Scriptures verses – via Brenda – that God had impressed on her heart for Stephen to read. She would also give them some thoughts, cautions and encouraging words that God laid on her heart. They treated her with such honor and respect. She believes God is going to "revolutionize" people through the movie *War Room*. Over the course of the next several weeks, through a couple more Skype sessions, my mom met and prayed for the lead actress, Priscilla Shirer. Her prayer was powerful and obviously moved Priscilla so much that a few weeks later she mentioned to Beth Moore (who has a cameo role in the movie) about this woman who prayed for her. Beth Moore wanted to meet my mom. It was surreal to see my mother sitting at my kitchen table in front of a computer, praying with and for Beth Moore. Although *War Room* is a team effort between all three Kendrick brothers, my mother simply refers to it as "Stephen's movie."

As a result of their newly-formed friendship, Stephen Kendrick asked if he could film an interview with her. We arranged an interview with her in her home a few months ago when he was going to be in Nashville for a few days. LifeWay's camera crew arrived a few hours before Stephen did. She watched with fascination as they took the time to light the home and arrange their furniture. She had never met Stephen. When he pulled up, you'd think she was meeting a long lost son or something. She hugged him and kissed him on the cheek and hugged him and kissed him again. She loves "her Stephen" and prays continually for him and his wife Jill. During the interview, Stephen asked her opinion of so many topics. It was awesome to see and hear her plain and simple holy wisdom. Being the proud mom she is, if she gets the chance to promote me or something I've done (or my husband or son or brother or any one of her grandchildren), she's going to take that chance. All through the interview she kept interjecting to Stephen that he needed "to hear a song my son-in-law wrote. It's called 'The Place of Prayer.' You should use it in your movie!" We didn't know she had elected herself our song-pitching agent. A few times during the interview, Stephen would ask her something, she would answer and then remind him that "You need to hear my son-in-law's song. It's about prayer. It's made for your movie!" and Stephen would nod kindly and then ask another question.

The transcript that follows is of the last few moments of Stephen Kendrick's interview with her. I am so grateful to him that I now have this keepsake of her and her power and her love. On the night he recorded it, I had no idea it would so soon become an important record of her words and thoughts about dying.

> SK: *Are you afraid to die?*
>
> MB: *No. No. In fact my husband and I were talking about it this morning. We were saying, "I wonder what our new home is going to be like?" Yeah. Yeah. But you know, talking about wanting to die, like, the other morning I woke up and (I just spoke) the words, "The way of the cross leads home." That's what came out of my mouth. So I didn't know it was a song. Marie, she has to hear all my stories in the morning. So I said, "Marie, Marie", I said, "you know what just came out of my mouth? The way of the cross leads home." She said, "Mommy, that's a song." So I said "Really?" So I looked it up and I found it: The Way of the Cross Leads Home. In there it says, "When I say farewell to this world." So I'm excited about it. I can't wait until I see that beautiful face. You see how I hugged you tonight? That's how I'm going to hug Jesus.*
>
> SK: *Amen. That's good. That's good. We love you.*
>
> MB: *I love you. I love you.*
>
> SK: *Thank you for doing this. Sharing you heart, loving the Lord, encouraging everyone whose listens to this. This has been an honor and a privilege to be able to meet with Miss Molly and we've gotten to spend a little bit of time with her and hopefully fall more in love with the Lord ourselves.*
>
> MB: *Yes.. amen.. amen.. Now do you want to hear my son-in-law's song?*

Stephen patiently obliged her. The camera crew gathered around the piano in my parents' home. Phil sat down and began to sing one of her favorite songs of all time - and not just because her son-in-law wrote it. (Well, not entirely.) Here are the lyrics:

There's a place that I know and whenever I go, I find peace in these troubled days. It's a place where God meets me, and then I'm aware of His Spirit.

It's the place of prayer. The place of prayer. Where untold blessing is found. The place of prayer. Where my riches abound. When I'm alone, and Jesus is there, that's where I find the place of prayer.

This place of prayer means so much to me, I meet Jesus whenever I'm on my knees. When trouble comes to move me, with worry and care, that's when I run to that place of prayer.

The place of prayer. Where untold blessing is found. The place of prayer. Where my riches abound. When I'm alone and Jesus is there, that's where I find, the place of prayer.[17]

Molly's Meatball Lesson #76

A day without prayer is a day without peace.

Resurrection. Really? Really.

*"Jesus said to her, 'I am the **resurrection** and the life. The one who believes in me will live, even though they die.'"*

— JOHN 11:25

As I write this, it has been six weeks since her diagnosis. She quoted John 11:25 to me this morning as she woke up. With her beautiful face smiling at me, with sleep still surrounding her, she spoke those words. They seem to come out of her innermost being, these promises of God.

Mom reminded me once again that we believe in the reality of resurrection. She said, "Marie, don't forget that Jesus said, '*Because I live, you also will live*' (John 14:19). He came to defeat death, Marie. At the moment I am facing death, He will be right there with me."

Throughout the years, Mom always aid to me, ""The cross is not the end of the story. The end of the story is being resurrected." It's too late to change the symbol of Christianity to an empty tomb like she suggested once. But in reality, it's the empty tomb that is the point of the cross. Putting my faith in what Jesus did on the cross is my life or death decision. Resurrection is freely given but we have to freely choose it.

"Marie, when you see them put me in the grave, please remember that someday it will be empty. It won't be long until He gives me my resurrected body." Yes, Mom. I will try to remember that.

Molly's Meatball Lesson #77

Jesus had the first tomb that stayed empty forever so that whosoever believes in Him will also have a tomb that stays empty forever.

Liar, Liar

"Jesus said to them – 'You belong to your father, the devil and you want to carry out your father's desires. He was a murderer from the beginning, not holding to the truth, for there is no truth in him. When he lies, he speaks his native language, for he is a liar and the father of lies. Yet because I tell the truth,

you do not believe me!'"

— JOHN 8:44-45

Today, eight weeks and one day since her diagnosis, Mom was speaking about the fact that when God created Adam, He "breathed into

his nostrils the breath of life, and the man became a living being."
(Genesis 2:7) She is fascinated by the fact that the first breath has been
breathed into every human since the Garden of Eden. She muses, "That
very breath of very God is what brought life to humanity. God doesn't
breathe death into people. He breathes life. His plan for us is life. We
have allowed ourselves to be robbed of the life God intended all along.
I think that God gives us His breath at the moment of creation and at
the moment our lives end, He simply takes His breath back and brings
us home."

Eve believed a lie. Satan painted a false picture of God. When Eve accepted his lie, she rejected truth. Just like in John 8, Jesus pointed out that
people are more willing to embrace a lie than accept the truth. All the evil
that we see, all the fear we live with, all the pain, all the sickness, all the
anger and lying, and jealousy, and lawlessness: that's what the human race
bought when Eve bought satan's lies. God doesn't cause it, our sin does.

You know, if Mom hadn't gotten this terminal diagnosis as I was
finishing up this book, I would probably not have ended this book
focused on her primary recipe for living: Life ends. She lived every
moment of every day focused on that fact. She knew without a doubt
her life would end. And she lived each day trying to remind others that
their lives would end also. She often quoted this verse: *"It is appointed
unto men once to die, but after this the judgment"* (Heb. 9:27, KJV). No one can
escape the death sentence. Ignoring it doesn't make it go away. Even as I
write about her fading away, I am also fading away. And so are you. And
there is nothing you can give to God in exchange for your eternal soul,
to pay for your sin. Someone has to pay for your sin. You cannot live
a good-enough life to resurrect your very soul. Neither can I. Neither
can my mom. Our only hope is in the blood of Jesus because it is full
payment for our sin. Honest.

Molly's Meatball Lesson #78

*As you're busy living your life, don't be too busy to think about your
afterlife.*

"Jesus, You Go First"

"A person's days are determined; you have decreed the number
of his months and have set limits he cannot exceed."

— JOB 14:5

When I started writing this book, I didn't expect that it would also include a short, unwelcomed section that could be titled "The Recipe For Dying My Mother Taught Me." And yet I have come to understand that this is a lesson — the last lesson - she needs to teach me. And teaching me she is. Yesterday she decided to tell me the story of the day her mother died. Nonnon simply died in her sleep. She was 85 years old. She wasn't ill. She just got old and went to sleep one night and died.

Yesterday, I was sitting by my own mom's bed before she went to sleep for the night and she just started to say, "You know, when my mother died, I was the one designated to deal with the funeral home. And the funeral director told me I had to go and get clothes for her to wear in the casket. As I drove to her house I prayed, 'Lord, I cannot go into that room and get Momma's clothes for her to wear in a casket. Lord, I cannot do it. The only way I can do it is if You go in that room first, if You go in before me and with me.' And so, when I got to the door of her bedroom, I stepped back and said, 'Jesus, please go first. I cannot go in there alone.' I waited as if to give Him time to enter her bedroom. And somehow I found the strength to do what I needed to do. I didn't cry. I just did it with Jesus and with His strength. And you will too, Marie. You will too."

And that was Mom's way of telling me what to do when I face the end of my mother's life. And with all things, that's exactly what I plan on doing: following Jesus as He walks before me. Following the example of following Jesus that my mother Molly lived.

Molly's Meatball Lesson #79

You'll be surprised to see what you can overcome in life if you remember that Jesus has already overcome it for you.

The Mom of All Comfort

"Praise be to the God and Father of our Lord Jesus Christ, the Father of compassion and the God of all comfort, who comforts us in all our troubles,
so that we can comfort those in any trouble with the comfort we ourselves receive from God."

— 2 CORINTHIANS 1:3-4

Mom's four sisters and their husbands and her two brothers and their wives have already departed this earth. These seven couples lived life together for many joy-filled decades. My parents are the only couple still alive.

My cousins cherish my parents, Aunt Molly and Uncle Joe, and have been very involved in supporting us through this painful process. My cousin Larry said to me, "Something that has been with me for almost 40 years and has affected me profoundly is the way your mother acted when Nonnon died. I remember everyone was in the room. They were wailing and crying and your mother was calm and quiet. She had peace. She said to everyone, 'Don't you understand that we are standing in the place where just a few minutes ago the Lord came and took Momma. She saw the face of Jesus. She is in His presence. Let's rejoice for her instead of crying. Jesus Himself was just in this room.'" Larry explained that seeing the reality of the hope my mother had, in the moment she had just lost her mother has reminded him for decades that her faith is real. And so is Jesus.

We have been living at their house for the past several weeks because they both need 24 hour a day, seven days a week care. My husband loves my parents as if they were his parents. That's because they both treated him like a son and not a son-in-law. I am so honored to care for them. I am so thankful for every second my mother is breathing breath on this side of eternity that I will do whatever it takes to keep her breathing. My mom, always thinking of others, has seen how much work is required to care for her and my dad at home. It is work but it is not a burden. Yesterday I overheard her praying, "Lord, have mercy on Phil and Marie and take me home. They can't keep living this way. They can't be expected to give up their lives just to take care of two old people. Lord, relieve them of this burden. Take us home."

Forgetting for a moment that she was a terminally ill woman, I actually scolded her, "Mom! Stop praying that way. You want the Lord to take your life just so Phil and I can relax? Are you kidding me, Mom? You are not a burden. Do we make you feel like you and Daddy are a burden?"

"No. No. Never!"

My emotions were spilling out as I said, "Then stop telling God that you are a burden. Oh, and while I'm telling you the truth, let me say this. We have never been false with one another and I'm not going to start now. It's true that I want God's will. And I have told you that I release you to Him, as if I have a vote in whether He calls you home. But I have to tell you that the real truth, the honest truth in the depth of my heart, is that I don't want you to leave. I don't want you to die. I don't care how happy you are going to be in the presence of the Lord. I want you here. I want you here with me. I cannot imagine my life without you, Mom. You are my best friend. I need you."

"I know, mommy's girl, I know."

And she let me cry on her shoulder. And she hugged me tight. And she wiped my tears away. And she said, "I have been praying for you and the Lord has assured me that you will be fine and that He will comfort you. And so you will be fine and the Lord will comfort you because He has never lied to me." Yesterday, I had to go the funeral home and choose her coffin and make burial arrangements. Phil stayed behind with my parents. I didn't tell her where I was going. I just explained I needed to go out. My son Philip met me at the funeral home for support. As I walked to the door of the funeral home, I said, "Lord, You see me going in to this place to choose my mother's coffin. Lord, I cannot believe I just said those words to You. I cannot believe this is happening. I cannot believe, Lord, that my mother is dying. How can this be? Lord, I don't think I have the strength to do this. But if You will walk into that funeral home before me, I will follow."

And I stopped at the door. And I waited for the Lord to walk in before me. And I walked in. I chose what needed to be chosen. And that was that. I wasn't happy about it. I had some moments when the emotions were overwhelming. But God gave me the strength to do it. I hugged my wonderful son, got in my car, and drove back to my parents' house. Phil looked at me to see how I was and I said, "I'm fine. I'm really fine." And I was fine. I was surprised at how fine I actually was.

Could Mom be right? Again? I went to my Mom's room and said, "Mom, I am going to do what you did when Nonnon died and ask Jesus to go before me as I have to walk through these difficult days. I know it's the only way I will get through it."

She smiled and nodded as she said, "And you will get through it."

Molly's Meatball Lesson #80

Today is the tomorrow you were worried about yesterday.
Live one day at time.

"I Have Peace"

"You will keep in perfect peace those whose minds are steadfast, because they trust in you."

— ISAIAH 26:3

It is Sunday, May 31, 2015, and last night Mom started to show signs that she is a terminally ill woman. She cannot keep anything in her stomach. She cannot drink. She cannot eat. However, we are still going to celebrate my granddaughter Rachel's 11th birthday today at their home. It's a family tradition that we gather at my parents' house to celebrate the birthday of each family member. The house is decorated with balloons and the number "11" hanging in front of the window. Mom is still alert, though tired. The decorations make her smile. She loves her family. The party begins and she and dad sit on the sofa with the family.

Our family's birthday season begins in October of each year and ends with Rachel's birthday in June. I am thinking about this as I watch her laughing with the family. She was here to celebrate everyone's birthday, her wedding anniversary in February, my birthday (the most important one, of course) in April, her birthday in May, Mother's Day, my father's birthday in May, and finally Rachel's birthday. She didn't miss one event. I whisper a "Thank You" to the Lord.

It is Tuesday, June 2, 2015. The hospice nurse was here yesterday but I call and ask her to come check Mom again today. Last night she couldn't sleep at all because she couldn't keep anything down. The nurse quietly says to me, "She can't really get any sicker than not being able to drink or eat." The nurse knows I am not seeing the full picture. I ask her, "How much time does she have?" She is reluctant to give an answer, explaining that each person is different. I ask a different way, "I know you don't know for sure, but if you had to guess, how long do you think my mother has?" She paused and said, "I would guess that she will be gone by the weekend." Weekend? Today is Tuesday. The weekend is just three days away.

It is Wednesday, June 3, 2015, exactly nine weeks since her diagnosis at Vanderbilt. Mom is sleeping most of the time. Our family is gathering around her. I walked into her room an hour ago and she was awake. "Mom," I asked, "Do you have pain?" She smiled and said, "No. I have peace." Peace. Yes, it's all over her face.

It is Thursday, June 4, 2015. She has not been awake much. I am swabbing her mouth with little sponges attached to lollipop sticks so that she gets some moisture in her mouth. She cannot speak above a whisper. I walked into her room and she was awake. Trying to be cheerful I said, "Whatcha doing, Mom?" She took her hand, placed it on her heart, and then lifted it toward the ceiling and said, "Waiting." She smiled. She's waiting for Jesus.

It is Friday, June 5, 2015. Mom is not conscious that often. I feel a wave of panic when I think that maybe I have spoken to her for the last time and didn't realize it. "Lord, please give me another chance to talk to Mom. Please let her wake up." My son, whom she adores, walked into her bedroom about 10 minutes after I prayed that prayer and said, "Mema! It's Philip!" She instantly opened her eyes. For the past hour or so she has been awake, and though her voice is a mere whisper, she whispers to me, "I love you so much." Those are the last words my mother ever spoke to me. And the last words I ever spoke to my mother that I am sure she heard were, "I love you too, Mom. The Lord is here and close to you."

All day Friday we sang songs, we read Scriptures and we held her hand and rubbed her arms. I slept in the recliner next to her bed while Renee stayed awake to keep vigil. She never awoke again. I promised my mother that I would never leave her side. And by the grace and mercy of God, He allowed me to keep that promise. And with the family she loved and the family who loved her gathered at her side, we waited for Jesus to come and bring my mother home. I held her hand and whispered in her ear that we were all there with her. And on Saturday, June 6, 2015, at 11:07 AM, as I held her hand, and my son held her other hand, as the family was gathered around her bed, gazing intently at this mother we so love, a heavenly escort arrived and took my mother home to the Love of her life. I cannot know what she saw. I just know she is in the presence of the Lord. I didn't see any angels. I didn't see any bright lights. All I saw was a woman of God, breathing slowly and peacefully until she took that one last breath. God took His breath back and took Molly Bruno home.

Precious Faithful Servant

"Precious in the sight of the Lord is the death of his faithful
servants."

— Psalm 116:15

As I write this it is four weeks since my mother was buried in her Resurrection Ground. It is four weeks and counting until I am reunited with her. I miss her. Mom's memorial service would have delighted her. My brother spoke, I spoke, Renee spoke. My husband Phil sang a song he had started years ago but competed in time for Mom to hear it. It speaks of a person who has lived their entire life waiting to hear just two words from Jesus: "Well done." It's beautiful. Our pastor had a tape recording of a phone call Molly had with him a few years ago. On the call she just kept talking and talking, sharing Scripture after Scripture. You could hear me in the background saying, "Ma! Let the pastor hang up!" The recording captured her essence completely and accurately. She was hilarious and holy all in one person. A young woman named Tracy got up to speak about my mom's life. Tracy's family lived two houses away from my parents when they lived in Staten Island. Coincidentally Tracy moved to Nashville and her parents followed her. They bought a house just a few houses away from my parents' house in Tennessee. Tracy shared so beautifully about how my mom's life changed the course of their whole family's life. Just one determined woman and one broken family in her "Jerusalem" that she refused to ignore. Tracy gave her life to Jesus and eventually so did her parents. I know that Tracy's story of how Mom reached out can be repeated hundreds and hundreds of times.

For example in an email to me, Renee's sister-in-law Leanne wrote the most beautiful words in an email to me about "Meems" (the name her great grandchildren use for her) and how Mom had affected her life. I asked Renee to read her words at the memorial service. Here's a portion of what she wrote: Leanne wrote, *"Dear Marie… Meems has left a lasting impact on my life and I treasure the things I learned from her. I'm gonna miss calling her when things are falling apart around me and listening to her pray for me and my family. She gave me hope when I would want to give up. She made me fight harder when it seemed impossible. She had a way of making me feel so special. Her love and trust for Jesus was amazing! The love and faith she had in Jesus was contagious! Meems loved everyone and it didn't matter your past she would always remind you, 'Jesus loves you, Leanne, Jesus loves you!' I remember when and where I was just like it was yesterday when Meems read me this verse. It's Ephesians 6:12 and it says, 'For we are not fighting against flesh-and-blood enemies, but against evil rulers and authorities of the unseen world, against mighty powers in this dark world, and against evil spirits in the heavenly places' (NLT). She opened up my eyes or heart I should say. You see when we have issues with a spouse, a child, a friend, our reaction is to attack or fight against that person. But Meems taught me it's not about the person. We need to pray for the person, pray for their soul. Satan is here to attack families, our marriage, our children, our relationships. From that day forward I saw things so differently. I hear her voice, 'Don't give up! Keep praying for the person or situation.' I praise the Lord for her life and the many she led to the Lord. I can only imagine the smile on her face when she saw her Jesus!"*

Another wonderful tribute to her that I read at the service came from Stephen Kendrick. She prayed so diligently for him and "his" movie. As a matter of fact, before they started filming, he asked if it would be possible to have some items from her home to include in the decorating of Miss Clara's home in the movie. I made a quick video of some items plus her Bible. He chose some plaques and pictures and asked if he could borrow her Bible. Mom said, "Sure!" All through the movie, Miss Clara is using Mom's Bible. In the very last scene of the movie, Miss Clara prays a powerful prayer and the scene begins with a close up of Mom's Bible. When Stephen heard about my mother's health, and we realized that she might not make it to the release date in August 2015, he arranged for her to have a DVD of the movie to see. She cried when she saw her Bible. She watched it two times and loved it. As she watched the movie, she was raising her hands and saying "Amen! Hallelujah!" Talking to the TV. Agreeing with so much of the dialogue you'd think she was at a revival meeting. She was crying and rejoicing and agreeing and laughing.

She said, "Stephen's movie is going to change hearts!" Stephen asked my mom would to call him after she saw the movie. It happens that he and Alex were together in the car. I listened as she said, "Stephen, I am so proud of you. I am so proud of you. You did not compromise God's Word. You did not water anything down. I am so proud of you and your movie. God is going to use your movie, Stephen. And use it mightily." I interrupted to say, "Alex, excuse my mom for referring to this as Stephen's movie." He laughed and said, "It's not a problem at all. Anyone who loves my brother loves me."

Here is what Stephen Kendrick wrote about my mother:

TRIBUTE TO OUR DEAR BELOVED FRIEND MOLLY BRUNO "UNINHIBITED"

One of the greatest treasures of my life during the past year has been the unexpected friendship of a 91-year-old, Italian prayer warrior named Molly Bruno.

When I heard about Molly's special relationship with the Lord, her unique prayer life, and her ongoing miraculous circumstances, I wanted to meet her personally. At the same time, we were in the process of writing the script for a movie, called War Room, *which was about the power of prayer and, of all things, featured a feisty, lovable old woman who really knew how to get a hold of God on her knees.*

When I finally met Molly, I considered it an inspired, divine appointment to see a living representation of the heart and faith we planned to show in the film. I heard about her God-given dreams helping her to know how to pray in light of coming events, her years of serving in ministry with her husband, Joseph, her continued witnessing adventures at Publix to the employees. Molly had me laughing, in tears, and held spellbound with the stories of answered prayer in her life and what it means to walk with God.

As I listened to her, my heart was full. Here is a short, white-haired, unassuming woman with a knowing smile on her face and a twinkle in her eye, who has spent countless thousands of hours in prayer, whose family members laugh at the seemingly endless supply of miraculous events connected to her life, and whose morning coffee with Jesus is a sacred daily appointment. She would often shed very tender tears as she talked with me about how much she loved her Savior. You cannot interact with Molly without sensing the love, joy, and presence of Christ residing in her. Spending time with her made me want to be a better man and to spend more time with the Lord myself.

After hearing about our next movie, War Room, *Molly decided to personally undergird the entire project and our efforts in prayer. From the writing, to the casting, to the filming, Molly was holding us up and interceding on our behalf. I vividly remember being at the production office in Concord, North Carolina, and seeing our lead actress, Priscilla Shirer, on her knees and in tears as she listened to Molly praying for her over the phone before we began the production.*

We used Molly's Bible in the film as the main Bible Miss Clara's prays with. When we stayed up late filming in North Carolina, Molly would stay up late and pray for us from her modest home in Tennessee.

Looking back, I can't help but thank the Lord for the unexpected, priceless blessing to work on a movie and a book about the power of prayer, and to have Him raise up one of the godliest and most prayerful women in our nation to intercede on our behalf the entire time. We completed the movie in March of 2015 and then finished The Battle Plan for Prayer *book on the evening of June 5. Molly passed into eternity in less than 24 hours on June 6.*

The word that comes to mind when I think of Molly is "uninhibited." The Bible talks about how Christ sets us free from guilt, shame, sin, and the bondage of this world. He delivers us from self-centeredness, pride, and the fear of man as we trust Him. He gives us life and life more abundantly beyond the boundaries or limitations accustomed to this world. The Bible says that in Him, "we have boldness and confident access through faith in Him" (Eph. 3:12, NASU).

Molly Bruno was not inhibited by her past or the worries of the world. She didn't care what other people thought, she was on a mission to love them, pray for them, and to tell them about Jesus. She lived full-throttle, wide-open, speaking boldy, loving freely, and worshiping God wholeheartedly. I am a better man because of her. Even though I knew her for only a year, I grew to love her more deeply than people I've known for decades. I miss her and am looking forward to seeing her in heaven one day. She will be close to the throne, smiling, worshiping, singing, and loving every minute of it...for all eternity.

The book of Hebrews talks about the hall of faith of men and women who served God with extraordinary faith and passion. Those unique warriors for God's kingdom were relentless in their pursuit of Him and of taking as many people to Christ as they could while they still have breath. Molly Bruno is definitely one of them. Of whom the world is not worthy.

For the skeptic who says that God is not real and prayer does not work, Molly's legacy stands as living proof that there is a powerful God in heaven who is involved in the affairs of men and works mightily on behalf of those who are willing to trust him.

As the Lord wills, we plan to release War Room *and* The Battle Plan for Prayer *all around the world to call people back to our Savior and back to their knees in prayer for our families, cities, and nations. Molly's investment in us and legacy of prayer will live on through the film and the book as they literally call millions of people to faith and faithfulness in Christ. Truly, "precious in the sight of the LORD is the death of His godly ones" (Ps. 116:15, NASU). Our condolences, prayers, and love go out to her dear family. Stephen Kendrick*

Mom asked that our son son Philip sing a beautiful worship song he wrote at her funeral. She sang it constantly. Mom sang it to anyone who called her. To honor this grandmother he adored, Philip took his guitar and sang these simple and powerful words: *"Lord, I trust in You. Lord,*

I trust in You. Whatever comes my way, I look to You and say 'Lord, I trust in You.'"18

Yes, that is the truth about my mom. My mom must have been rejoicing in heaven to hear that song and then to see that Philip is the one who preached the sermon at her funeral. Glorious? Preaching at her funeral? Hallelujah. As I watched my son speaking, I thought to myself that he looked exactly like the anointed man of God she always believed he was and is.

We closed the service with a recording of a voice mail she left on our home phone many years ago. She said, "I'm going to sing you a song." And then she sang, *"Open your heart and let Him in. God will remove all your sorrow and sin. He may not pass your way again, so open your heart and let Him come in. Take His hand. Take His nail-scarred hand. Let Him show the way. Jesus will be your dearest Friend. So, open your heart and let Him come in."19* Those words summed up her life. We ended the service, buried my beautiful mother, and turned our attention toward the other love of her life: my father.

Four Weeks and Counting

The day after my mom's burial, Phil and I took my father Joseph, 91, to live with us in our home. He has a cheerful room, painted yellow, and his adjustable bed is right next to a window overlooking beautiful trees. He's a kind and compassionate man. Never complains. He is my hero. Always has been. Always will be.

It took Dad a day or two to get used to the change but he seems to be pretty happy. And yet, in spite of the fact that his only illness is some light dementia, he is going through the process of his body shutting down. His hospice nurse has suggested mere weeks. His body just seems to have decided it's time to go home also.

People told me to expect this when a couple has been married as long as they have, which happens to be 72 years. My mom quoted the verse, *"He…. taketh away the understanding of the aged"* (Job 12:20, KJV) as explanation for Dad's forgetfulness. For the past four weeks, he has asked from time to time where Mom is. We would gently remind him that she was with the Lord. But two hours later, he'd forget and ask again. However, about two weeks ago, he asked me once again where Mom was. I said, "Daddy, Mommy is with the Lord." I could see it registering in his mind.

He said, "She died?"

"Yes, Daddy, she died and is with the Lord."

"So I don't have to take care of her anymore?"

"No, Daddy she is perfectly taken care of by Jesus."

Of all the things I want to do in life, telling my dad that his wife of 72 years has died is not at the top of my list. His main concern has always been to take care of Mommy. And I think that ever since that day, he has wanted to be absent in his body and present with the Lord. Just like Mom is. I love my dad. I am a daddy's girl.

I cannot say I have not had desperate prayers of asking Jesus to help my desperation. I cannot say that the big aching hole that is still very tender inside me has healed. I miss my mom. I realize that when a 92-year-old woman's life ends, it's just the way life is. It is sad but it isn't a tragedy. It's life. She lived to a long, happy, blessed and contented life. She did. That fact doesn't help me to stop missing her. I miss her.

Cards From Heaven?

For the first few days after she died, I was extremely and utterly sad and extremely and utterly thankful at the same time. My one request of the Lord when I first learned of her illness was that she would not suffer and that she would have a gentle departure. As I was going through it, I didn't know how it would end. I didn't know what tomorrow would bring. Would it bring a new complication? But when it ended I saw that God had mercifully answered my prayer. All through those 10 weeks, my mother was weak but didn't really suffer. And her passing was as peaceful as a newborn baby sleeping. So I miss her but I have so much to thank God for and about.

But let's get real. I have had days of utter sadness. In the days and weeks after she left, I was just hurting deeply inside. I did what Mom taught me to do. I ran to Jesus. "Help, Jesus! Help me. I miss mom, Jesus. I miss my mom! Help!" And He did. I mentioned in an earlier chapter, every day my mom would read her Bible and a verse would jump out to her. She would write that verse down on a plain white index card and it would become her "verse of the day." That verse would be the exact verse God would use to minister to someone who crossed her path. I have boxes filled with those cards. I know I will read them again and again. A few days after her funeral, I had to go out. It was a very sad day for me. I could not find comfort anywhere. I just wanted my mom and I wanted her now. I walked to the garage, got in the car, and sitting right in the middle of the passenger's seat was one of her index cards. Just one. There was her familiar handwriting and the card said, "Psalm 27:14 'Wait on the Lord: be of good courage and <u>He</u> shall strengthen thine heart: Wait, I say, on the Lord'" (KJV). "What?" I wondered, "What is this card doing here?" She had underlined the word "He." I assumed Phil put it there to encourage me. I went inside and asked him, "Did you put this card on the passenger seat in my car?" He looked at the card, "No. I saw it there and I thought you put it there. You didn't?" I didn't. Hmmm. How did it get there? I asked Philip, Renee. No one put it there. For sure the verse is exactly what I needed to read. The words "be of good courage" also mean "be brave, be strong." Buck up. God will help you. The verse is reminding me not to get impatient if God doesn't move as fast as I want Him to. God will strengthen me in my innermost place – my heart. He will? He will. I didn't want to get all weird and stuff, but I did think, "Mom, did you put that card there?" I just thanked the Lord for His Word and went on with my day. I got home later and was putting groceries away in the refrigerator. You can't really see the surface of the refrigerator because it is covered with magnets holding up pictures of my grandchildren and their drawings. I noticed something I hadn't noticed before. It was a white index card with my mother's handwriting and one of her verses. I stopped to read the verse. It was the same verse – Psalm 27:14 - that was on the seat of my car. I checked the car to see if maybe I'd brought the first card in and put it on the refrigerator and didn't remember doing it. The first card was still there. This was a second card with the same verse. The Lord was reminding me again through His Word that I should have courage and believe that He will strengthen my heart. It's what my mother told me that day I lost it: "The Lord has assured me that you will be fine and that He will comfort you. And so, you will be fine and the Lord will comfort you." And you know what? She was right. I am fine and the Lord is comforting me. I will never stop missing Molly Bruno. I will never fail to remember that I will see her again. And she will see me. "Thanks Mom, for making sure we spend forever together. I love you."

Oh, one more thing. When I was a young girl, my mom told me she'd had a dream that she went to be with the Lord on July 13th. She soon apologized for telling me about that dream because every year on July 13th I would worry that I was going to lose my mom. As she has been ill these last several months, we both wondered if her dream might have been accurate. As it turns out, it was not accurate for her. However, it was accurate for my sweet father. On July 13, 2015 just thirty-seven days after Mom went to be with the Lord, dad died peacefully in his sleep. He was taking no medication for any illness. He just went to be with Mom. "Thanks Dad for making sure we all spend eternity together. I love you."

Molly's Final Meatball Lesson To Me

The Lord will never leave me, even when my mother and father do.

12

IT'S NOT BY CHANCE YOU READ THIS BOOK

A Message From Molly

"For God so loved the world that he gave his one and only Son, that whoever believes in him shall not perish but have eternal life. For God did not send his Son into the world to condemn the world, but to save the world through him."

— JOHN 3:16-17

Because it soon became obvious that my mother would not be here to comment on this book after it came out, I asked her what she would like to say to people who might read it.

Here's her response:

"It's not by chance you read this book. God had you read this book so that you would know that Jesus loves you. You may think you read this book because you want to know about Molly Bruno, but the reason you read this book is because God wants you to know about Jesus. It's Jesus who brings life. It's Jesus who brings joy. It's Jesus who brings peace. No matter how much you like what my daughter wrote

about me, the only thing that matters about me is that Jesus mattered to me. I pray that through something you read in this book, the Holy Spirit would reveal to you that the love you are looking for can only be found in Jesus. You may have had the best mother in the world, but without Jesus, you feel empty. Without Jesus, you are still searching. You may not have had a mother who loved you and you keep looking for a mother figure to love you the way you should have been loved. I will tell you that the love you are searching for can only be found by finding Jesus. You may have ruined your life with failure but Jesus loves you just the way you are, right now as you are reading this. If you offer the simplest prayer to Him, if it comes from your heart, He will hear and He will answer. Other people may have abused you but Jesus is able to resurrect the deadness that is your heart and bring you back to life. Church people may have let you down, but Jesus never will.

I know that God is real. I know that He answers prayer. I know that He speaks to us and walks with us and cares about us. I know that He cares about you. He does.

If just one person who reads this book decides to put their faith in Jesus and to live the rest of their days following Him, then my whole life has been worth it all. They tell me my life will be over soon. I am ready. Are you? Do you know that you have no guarantee that you will see tomorrow?

I cannot bear the thought that someone reading this book is someone who might be spending eternity separated from God. Jesus loves you so much that He died to conquer the death I am now getting ready to face. I am not afraid. He is with me. Don't fear death. Find life in Jesus.

Listen to me. Don't put this book down assuming it's just something that happened to be in front of you. God Himself allowed you to read this book so that you would know that Jesus loves you. It's not by chance you read this book."

Molly Bruno
May 7, 2015

Molly's Meatball Lesson #1
Honoring God means accepting yourself the way God created you. It also means accepting your children the way God created them and teaching your children to accept how God created them.

Molly's Meatball Lesson #2
Jesus is your advocate supporter who is in heaven right now, pleading your case before God Himself. So lighten up about the mistake thing.

Molly's Meatball Lesson #3
When you make a mistake, admit it. Seek forgiveness for it. Forgive others the way you've been forgiven. And then "fuggheddabboudit."

Molly's Meatball Lesson #4
You are more than qualified to do more than you can imagine if you acknowledge that you can only do it through Christ (Phil. 4:13).

Molly's Meatball Lesson #5
Don't be afraid to ask God to do whatever you want Him to do as long as you are willing to accept whatever He decides to do.

Molly's Meatball Lesson #6

Prayer must have its basis in love. Love for the one you are praying for. Love for the One you are praying to.

Molly's Meatball Lesson #7

The primary purpose of prayer is telling Someone who loves you more than anything that you love Him the same way.

Molly's Meatball Lesson #8

A fake prayer is a waste of your time and God's.

Molly's Meatball Lesson #9

If God alone is not reward enough for you then nothing else ever will be.

Molly's Meatball Lesson #10

Praying to God about your every day cares and needs – big or small - is the way your children and others will learn that God cares about their every day cares and needs – big or small.

Molly's Meatball Lesson #11

Don't teach your children to expect God to perform a miracle every day, but don't forget to let them know when He does.

Molly's Meatball Lesson #12

Let your children see and hear you asking God for what seems impossible. It's the only way they will learn for themselves that with God nothing is impossible.

Molly's Meatball Lesson #13

If God is a real and living and ever present help in times of trouble in **your** everyday life, He will be a real and living every present help in times of trouble in the everyday lives of your children, your family, your neighbors and everyone who knows you.

Molly's Meatball Lesson #14

Don't start shaking when the world starts shaking. Heaven never has a national emergency. And prayer is always the only solution.

Molly's Meatball Lesson #15

Your children will learn to pray from the prayers they hear at home more than the prayers they hear at church.

Molly's Meatball Lesson #16

If prayer is your first response in every situation, it will become your children's first response in every situation.

Molly's Meatball Lesson #17

Where there's a will, there's a witness. It's always God's will for you to witness about Jesus.

Molly's Meatball Lesson #18

If you want your children to focus on the things that matter to God, you have to first focus on the things that matter to God.

Molly's Meatball Lesson #19

Everywhere you go is a mission field, your Jerusalem. Everyone you know is a mission field, especially your own children.

Molly's Meatball Lesson #20

Just because some people reject the gospel doesn't mean you should stop preaching it.

Molly's Meatball Lesson #21

Almost everyone you meet is someone separated from God. Remember this. All day. Every day. Everywhere.

Molly's Meatball Lesson #22

If you want your children to be real in front of God and others, they need to see you being real in front of God and others.

Molly's Meatball Lesson #23

The best way to teach your children to witness is to let them see you doing it.

Molly's Meatball Lesson #24

Don't let the storms of your life keep you from telling others about Jesus.

Molly's Meatball Lesson #25

If you ask God to send people your way who need to hear about His love, He will send them. Never waste an opportunity to say, "Jesus loves you."

Molly's Meatball Lesson #26

If you don't pray for the people you know who don't know Jesus – who will?

Molly's Meatball Lesson #27
There is no age limit on memorizing Scripture. Do it with your children and your grandchildren. And keep doing it until you see the Lord.

Molly's Meatball Lesson #28
Read the Bible. Then do what it says.

Molly's Meatball Lesson #29
Read the Bible like it's a love letter from God Himself. Because that's exactly what it is.

Molly's Meatball Lesson #30
Live the Bible more than you quote it.

Molly's Meatball Lesson #31
Jesus died for your sin whether you believe that or not.

Molly's Meatball Lesson #32
Don't expect to be an expert at everything. Know your own limitations. There's nothing wrong with acknowledging that some tasks are better left to others.

Molly's Meatball Lesson # 33
Don't assume you will see tomorrow. Live each day as if it is your last because it might be.

Molly's Meatball Lesson #34
Always remember that if you are a child of God, God's power walks in to every room that you walk in to. Every other power must bow to the power of God within you.

Molly's Meatball Lesson #35
If you did it, admit it.

Molly's Meatball Lesson #36
The best way to deal with people laughing at your mistakes is to laugh along with them.

Molly's Meatball Lesson #37
Teaching a child that parents deserve honor is not an option. It's a commandment.

Molly's Meatball Lesson #38
If you're too busy to care for and about your own parents, you're too busy.

Molly's Meatball Lesson #39
Honor your father, especially if your father honors the Lord.

Molly's Meatball Lesson #40
It's very likely that the way your treat your parents is the way your children will treat you.

Molly's Meatball Lesson #41
If you can't say something nice about your parents, don't say anything at all.

Molly's Meatball Lesson #42
Honoring your parents is an everyday event. Do it every day. And make it an event.

Molly's Meatball Lesson #43
A child who will blatantly disobey a parent will have no fear of blatantly disobeying God.

Molly's Meatball Lesson # 44
A miserable marriage is never God's idea.

Molly's Meatball Lesson #45
Two people who think they know how marriage works better than the One who created it are two people who don't know the One who created marriage.

Molly's Meatball Lesson #46
Your husband's reputation is formed by the words of your mouth. Be careful with it.

Molly's Meatball Lesson #47
Don't let the kids take priority all the time. First you were a wife. Every now and then take the time to keep first things first.

Molly's Meatball Lesson #48
If you don't pray for your family, who will? Pray. Pray. And then pray some more.

Molly's Meatball Lesson #49
No woman ever ruined her marriage by taking time to look good for her husband.

Molly's Meatball Lesson #50
A wife who unwilling to forgive her husband's mistakes is making a bigger mistake than the mistake she is unwilling to forgive.

Molly's Meatball Lesson #51

The world is filled with people who refuse to see themselves honestly. Don't assume you aren't one of them.

Molly's Meatball Lesson #52

Storms are part of life on earth. In an instant, Jesus can calm every storm.

Molly's Meatball Lesson #53

Remind your children of the eternal and royal identity every Christian possesses.

Jesus wore a crown of thorns so that His children could wear crowns of gold.

Molly's Meatball Lesson #54

Don't say no all the time, but say it without hesitating when no is the right thing to say to your child.

Molly's Meatball Lesson #55

When disciplining your children, use your "or else" sentences sparingly. The only thing worse than your child not obeying you is you not doing what you said you would do if your child did not obey.

Molly's Meatball Lesson #56

God never uses His power and authority to exasperate His children. He isn't really happy with parents who do.

Molly's Meatball Lesson #57

If you want your child to marry a believer, it's never too soon to pray for and about their future spouse. And get your children to pray for them too.

Molly's Meatball Lesson # 58

Let God decide when and how your child needs to endure the thorns of life. As a parent, do your best to remove the thorns you are able to.

Molly's Meatball Lesson #59

The biggest mistake a parent can make is telling your child he was a mistake. Don't do it.

Molly's Meatball Lesson #60

Our Heavenly Father never makes us feel like He sacrificed too much in order to have us as His child. Don't ever make your child feel like you have sacrificed too much to be a parent.

Molly's Meatball Lesson #61

Talk to and about your children the way you'd like your children to talk to and about you.

Molly's Meatball Lesson #62

Choose your parenting battles. Don't be a cop. If the crime is small, and your child doesn't know you've seen them break a small rule, then look away. Let it go.

Molly's Meatball Lesson #63

Keep your burdens to yourself - unless you are giving them to Jesus. He has the strength to carry every burden. Your children do not.

Molly's Meatball Lesson #64

As long as you accept that you never know it all, then you will always be willing to inquire of the One who does.

Molly's Meatball Lesson #65

Don't assume you know the whole story of someone else's life. You never know. But God does. Pray.

Molly's Meatball Lesson #66

Just because you feel like talking about something doesn't mean you should. When staying on a subject is causing division or sin – get off that subject.

Molly's Meatball Lesson #67

Having the right to do something doesn't mean you should do it. Your actions must always be the actions of Jesus.

Molly's Meatball Lesson #68

Don't waste time pointing out your flaws to God. Instead thank Him for Jesus. In Him you are completely beautiful and righteous.

Molly's Meatball Lesson #69

A Christian who doesn't understand that God's plan is to make her look and act like Jesus, is a Christian who will never comprehend why God is allowing what God is allowing.

Molly's Meatball Lesson #70

Just because someone says God told her to tell you something doesn't mean that God told her to tell you something.

Molly's Meatball Lesson #71
Don't expect God to speak to you in dreams and visions, but don't expect Him not to.

Molly's Meatball Lesson #72
Just because someone just told you that you're dying is no reason to forget they are dying too. Make sure they know Jesus.

Molly's Meatball Lesson #73
The Kingdom of God is not a democracy. God is not required to explain.

Molly's Meatball Lesson #74
The best way to keep from being discouraged is to keep encouraging others.

Molly's Meatball Lesson #75
Being thankful is always possible. Praise will bring peace.

Molly's Meatball Lesson #76
A day without prayer is a day without peace.

Molly's Meatball Lesson #77
Jesus had the first tomb that stayed empty forever so that whosoever believes in Him will also have a tomb that stays empty forever.

Molly's Meatball Lesson #78
As you're busy living your life, don't be too busy to think about your afterlife.

Molly's Meatball Lesson #79
You'll be surprised to see what you can overcome in life if you remember that Jesus has already overcome it for you.

Molly's Meatball Lesson #80
Today is the tomorrow you were worried about yesterday. Live one day at time.

Molly's Final Meatball Lesson To Me
The Lord will never leave me, even when my mother and father do.

[1] http://listverse.com/2009/05/11/15-fascinating-facts-about-salt/.

[2] http://www.himalayancrystalsalt.com/salt-history.html.

[3] http://www.pewsocialtrends.org/2014/04/08/
after-decades-of-decline-a-rise-in-stay-at-home-mothers/.

[4] http://www.deseretnews.com/top/701/1/Rebecca-Woolf-10-of-the-
most-popular-women-bloggers-in-the-US-.html.

[5] www.barna.org/barna-update/millennials/635-5-reasons-millennials-
stay-connected-to-church#.U0lqZ8c-Icg.

[6] www.barna.org/barna-update/millennials/635-5-reasons-millennials-
stay-connected-to-church#.U0lqZ8c-Icg.

[7] http://www.webmd.com/fitness-exercise/
human-growth-hormone-hgh.

[8] Name changed.

[9] Psalm 56:8.

[10] http://demog.berkeley.edu/~andrew/1918/figure2.html.

[11] http://en.wikipedia.org/wiki/Staten_Island.

[12] http://en.wikipedia.org/wiki/Outerbridge_Crossing.

[13] http://www.silive.com/specialreports/index.ssf/2011/03/the_goethals_
bridge_674500_veh.html.

[14] https://sites.google.com/site/maryhmccarthy/
verrazano-narrowsbridge.

[15] U.S. Census/2012: Los Angeles (city limits)- 3,858,000; Chicago –
2,715,000; Dallas – 1, 241,000; Boston – 636,479.

[16] "He Has Forgiven Me," Words and Music by Marie Armenia ©1995
Penny Hill Publishing.

[17] Words and music by Phil Armenia, ©1973 Penny Hill Publishing/A.S.C.A.P.

[18] Words and music by Philip Armenia, Jr., © 2013 Penny Hill
Publishing/A.S.C.A.P.

[19] Words and music by Tim Spencer.

Made in the USA
Lexington, KY
26 November 2015